Bamat

Base
Christian
Communities
and
Social Change
in Brazil

Base
Christian
Communities
and
Social Change
in Brazil

W. E. Hewitt

University of Nebraska Press

Lincoln and London

The paper in this book meets the minimum
requirements of American National Standard for
Information Services—Permanence of Paper for Printed
Library Materials, ANSI Z39.48—1984.

Acknowledgments for the use of previously published
material appear on page xiii.

Publication of this book was assisted by a grant from
The Andrew W. Mellon Foundation.

Library of Congress Cataloging-in-Publication Data

Hewitt, W. E. (Warren Edward), 1954–
Base Christian communities and social change in
Brazil / W. E. Hewitt.
p.   cm.
Includes bibliographical references and index.
ISBN 0-8032-2356-0 (alk. paper)
1. Basic Christian communities—Brazil.   2. Catholic
Church—Brazil—History—1965–   3. Brazil—Church
history.   I. Title.
BX2347.72.B6H48   1991
250'.981—dc20   90-24025
                                         CIP

For Sara,
Christopher,
and Bess
and in memory
of Derek,
a special friend
with whom
I came to know
and love
Brazil and her
people

Contents

Preface

In recent years, as part of a newfound commitment to progressive social transformation, the Roman Catholic Church has become increasingly involved in the politics of confrontation and change at the level of society. This is perhaps nowhere more true than in Latin America. Here, the Church, very frequently in direct opposition to State authority, has over the years come to adopt the reform cause of the socially disadvantaged as its very own. In many countries (although by no means all), the pursuit of this end has meant nothing less than a complete transformation of the local Church from stalwart supporter of the status quo to active player in the defense of civil and human rights.

One regional institution that has pushed very hard for social change on the domestic front is the Roman Catholic Church of Brazil—a fact that has certainly not escaped the notice of interested observers within social-scientific and religious circles alike. Indeed, once considered synonymous with wealth and privilege, the Brazilian Church has come to be viewed as one of the most politically progressive Churches in all of Catholicism, owing to the uncompromising position it has taken in favor of the poor and oppressed.

Of particular interest to students of recent Church change in Brazil—or elsewhere, for that matter—are the *comunidades eclesiais de base* (ecclesial communities of the base), commonly referred to as CEBs. Although such groups are not exclusive to Brazil, they have flourished here more than anywhere else in the region. Predominantly lay, lower-class, and often politically oriented, the CEBs are frequently seen as the most visible expression of the Brazilian Church's newfound commitment to the masses. To many, they are a renovating force that will have an irreversible impact on both Roman Catholicism and Brazilian society generally.

Since at least 1974, a number of important works have emerged that attempt to chronicle and analyze the emergence of the CEB phenomenon. Some of these have offered more general treatments of the CEBs and other grass-roots movements as part of discussions about broader change within Brazilian Catholicism. These include Thomas Bruneau's *Political Trans-formation of the Brazilian Catholic Church* (1974), his *Church in Brazil* (1982), Madeleine Adriance's *Opting for the Poor: Brazilian Catholicism in Transition* (1986), and Scott Mainwaring's *Catholic Church and Poli-tics in Brazil, 1916–1985* (1986), as well as various works published in Portuguese, such as Luiz Gonzaga de Souza Lima's *Evolução política dos Católicos e da Igreja no Brasil* (1979), Marcio Moreira Alves's *A Igreja e a política no Brasil* (1979), Roberto Romano's *Brasil: Igreja contra estado* (1979), and Paulo Krischke and Mainwaring's *A Igreja nas bases em tempo de transição, 1974–1985* (1986).

Numerous other works have focused more squarely on the CEBs per se. More recent studies of this type include Marcello de Azevedo's *Basic Ecclesial Communities in Brazil* (1987), Adelina Baldissera's *CEBs: Poder, nova sociedade* (1988), and a small but growing collection of articles writ-ten by social scientists such as Bruneau (1986), Ana Maria Doimo (1989), and Mainwaring (1989). There also exists voluminous material on the CEBs both in Portuguese and in translation, originating from within the theology of liberation and authors such as Frei Betto, Alvaro Barreiro, and Leonardo Boff.

In spite of the existence of this now-abundant literature, however, far too little has been written, in a thoroughly comprehensive, empirical sense, about what the CEBs, in all their fundamental respects, actually are and do. The more general studies of the Brazilian Church prepared by Bruneau or Mainwaring, for example, deal only to a limited extent with the nature and success of the CEBs as part of a broader research agenda. For their part, some of the ostensibly more focused social-scientific examinations of the CEBs appearing in journals and edited volumes have tended to paint the organizations with a fairly broad brush, and others have dealt only with more specific aspects of group life, such as activities, or the CEBs' relation-ship to the institutional Church. Moreover, Church-based authors, who collectively have produced the greatest number of book- and article-length CEB studies, often appear to be concerned less with empirical description and more with the theological significance of the CEBs. Their primary ob-jective, it would seem, is to situate the CEBs within the larger mission of the Church, and often they are concerned as much with promoting the groups as with simply describing them. Even some of the more social-scientific work of Adriance, Azevedo, and Baldissera, who have attempted to provide a relatively dispassionate portrait of the groups, is colored by a certain empathy with the CEBs' social and political goals.

This book was written in an attempt to fill what appears, then, to be a significant gap in the current CEB literature, insofar as its principal aim is to provide a critical, comprehensive, and detailed empirical analysis of the CEB phenomenon as it exists today in Brazil. Based on data I collected during field-research trips to Brazil in 1984 and 1988, it investigates the CEBs' origins, examines the groups' essential nature and organization, and assesses the CEBs' present and potential sociopolitical impact, all from a purely social-scientific point of view.

Throughout the book's nine chapters, I argue that the CEBs must be understood first and foremost as a phenomenon born wholly within the institutional Church during a particular historical moment. I also reveal the groups, partly as a consequence of their origins, to be far more organizationally and orientationally complex than frequently imagined and thus to be affecting the course of social and political change in Brazil much more subtly and indirectly than many have held. I conclude the book with a consideration of the ways in which the very real gains the CEBs have made are currently imperiled by the present political crises within both Brazil and Roman Catholicism.

The portrait of CEB life and activation that the study reveals is informed primarily by an investigation of 22 groups in the southeastern Brazilian archdiocese of São Paulo. This research was conducted before the dismantling of this ecclesiastical unit undertaken by the Vatican in March 1989. Before it was reduced to its central core, São Paulo provided an excellent location for a study of the CEBs because of its geographic size and population (over 13 million) and the large number and vitality of the groups known to exist there.

The CEBs under study here were selected following a stratified-random sampling plan and examined over a four-year period using questionnaires, interviews, and participant observation. This material was liberally supplemented with available secondary studies of CEBs both in São Paulo and in various other parts of Brazil. A detailed description of the research plan, sample-selection procedure, and research instruments appears in the Appendix.

Obviously, a study of this magnitude could not have been conducted without the help of a number of people and organizations, in both Brazil and Canada. I should like to express my gratitude, first of all, to the

Brandãos of São Paulo, my adoptive Brazilian family. Marco and Célia Brandão, in particular, have been lifelong friends, and were the first to introduce me to Brazil and her people.

Special thanks are due, as well, to several individuals at the curia of the archdiocese of São Paulo. The late Father José Albanez introduced me to the inner workings of the local Church and provided me with invaluable information about the São Paulo CEBs. I am grateful also to Cardinal Archbishop Paulo Evaristo Arns and the bishops of the nine episcopal regions for consenting to some rather lengthy interviews and for providing me with abundant information on Church activities within their areas of jurisdiction. I am also eternally in debt to the scores of priests, nuns, and laypeople who, with few exceptions, gave freely of their time in an effort to provide me with a clear understanding of the nature and significance of the CEB phenomenon.

In addition to Church-based personnel, countless librarians and clerks at several agencies in São Paulo helped me to locate and wade through a good deal of background information. Among those places I visited most frequently were the following: the Biblioteca Central at the Pontifícia Universidade Católica, the Biblioteca dos Dominicanos, the Centro Brasileiro de Análise e Planejamento, the Centro Pastoral Vergueiro, the offices of the Conferência Nacional dos Bispos do Brasil, the Arquivo da Cúria, the offices of O São Paulo, the Instituto Brasileiro de Geografia e Estatística, Secretaria Municipal de Planejamento/Departamento de Informações, Empresa Metropolitana de Planejamento da Grande São Paulo, Secretaria Municipal de Famílias e Bem-Estar Social, and the Tribunal Regional Eleitoral.

In Canada, a host of sources provided financial assistance for the study in the form of grants and bursaries. These included an International Research and Development Centre travel grant, Doctoral and Ontario Graduate Scholarships from the federal and provincial governments, respectively, and various research and travel grants from a number of institutions, including McMaster University, the University of Lethbridge, and the University of Western Ontario. I also wish to express my gratitude to a number of individuals who have made invaluable contributions or offered their support during the course of my research on the Brazilian Church, including Reg Bibby, Robert and Ruth Blumstock, Howard Brotz, Tom Bruneau, Scott Mainwaring, Sara Macdonald Hewitt, and various friends and relatives, among them Catherine Janzen, John and Carole Hewitt, Colin and Patty Rowland, Marg Foster, Jim Hewitt, and Marg, Bob, and Sandy Macdonald.

Finally, though this book represents an original work in the social-scientific study of the CEB phenomenon, it draws occasionally and synthetically on work that I have previously published in the field and that must be acknowledged. Brief sections of chapter 2 have appeared in similar form in "The Preferential Option for the Poor in the Archdiocese of São Paulo," *Canadian Journal of Latin American and Caribbean Studies* 12 (May 1987): 75–88; and parts of chapter 7 in "Strategies for Social Change Employed by Comunidades Eclesiais de Base (CEBs) in the Archdiocese of São Paulo," *Journal for the Scientific Study of Religion* 25 (March 1986): 16–30. In addition, brief parts of chapters 1, 7, and 8 are rooted in discussions appearing in "Origins and Prospects of the Option for the Poor in Brazilian Catholicism," *Journal for the Scientific Study of Religion* 28 (June 1989): 120–35; and "Religion and the Consolidation of Democracy in Brazil: The Role of the Comunidades Eclesiais de Base (CEBS)," *Sociological Analysis: A Journal in the Sociology of Religion* 51 (Summer 1990): 139–52.

Abbreviations

BCCC	Brazil-Canada Chamber of Commerce
CAPDH	Comissão Arquidiocesana de Pastoral dos Direitos Humanos
CEAS	Centro de Estudo e Ação Social
CEB	Comunidade eclesial de base
CEBRAP	Centro Brasileiro de Análise e Planejamento
CERIS	Centro de Estatística Religiosa e Investigações Sociais
CIMI	Conselho Indigenista Missionário
CNBB	Conferência Nacional dos Bispos do Brasil
DIEESE	Departamento Intersindical de Estudos e Estatísticas Sócio-Econômicas
EMPLASA	Empresa Metropolitana de Planejamento da Grande São Paulo
FIBGE	Fundação Instituto Brasileiro de Geografia e Estatística
GESP	Governo do Estado de São Paulo
IBGE	Instituto Brasileiro de Geografia e Estatística
IUPERJ	Instituto Universitario de Pesquisas do Rio de Janeiro
LADOC	Latin American Documentation
MEB	Movimento de Educação na Base
MR-8	Movimento Revolucionário 8 de Outubro
MS	Minimum salary
OMI	Oblatos da Maria Imaculada
PCB	Partido Comunista Brasileiro
PC do B	Partido Comunista do Brasil
PDS	Partido Democrático Social
PDT	Partido Democrático Trabalhista
PFL	Partido da Frente Liberal
PJCP	Pontifícia Comissão Justiça e Paz

PMDB	Partido do Moviminto Democrático Brasileiro
PMSP	Prefeitura do Município de São Paulo
PT	Partido dos Trabalhadores
PTB	Partido Trabalhista Brasileiro
SEADE	Sistema Estadual de Análise de Dados
SEDOC	Serviço de Documentação
TFP	Tradição, Família, Propriedade

Introduction

Within the Roman Catholic Church, few lay movements in recent memory have attracted as large a following in such a short period of time as have the base Christian communities (comunidades eclesiais de base), or CEBs, as they are commonly known. During the second half of the 20th century, the groups have sprung up in middle-class and socially disadvantaged sectors of society in countries throughout the Catholic world.

More than anywhere else, however, the success of the CEBs is evident in Latin America, where there are reported to be well over 200,000 groups in operation. In the rural areas of this region, in countries such as El Salvador and Nicaragua, the CEBs have served as important nuclei of resistance to authoritarian regimes. Similarly, in the slums of large urban centers such as Lima and Santiago, they have been instrumental in organizing the poor for self-help purposes and in lobbying local and national governments for change.

In the growing literature on this emergent global phenomenon, the base communities are most commonly viewed as a special category of Catholic lay group. Thus, although they are seen as frequently engaging in explicitly this-worldly activities, they are nevertheless perceived as fundamentally religious entities operating within the larger structure of the Church. Some authors have even gone so far as to argue that the CEBs *are* the Church, or at least are becoming the Church, much as it was in its original state—in the Holy Land following the Crucifixion or in the Roman catacombs.

Though such a claim may be disputed, certainly in Brazil the CEBs maintain an unmistakable presence within the institution. It is likely here that the first CEBs were born and nurtured, and here where today there exist far more CEBs than in any other country. Estimates of their current strength, in fact, run as high as 80,000 to 100,000 groups.

Within this large body of Brazilian CEBs, most—although certainly not all—are formed of the poor and working classes. Typically, they count between 20 and 50 members, but some claim to attract up to 200. Usually, however, this larger figure includes those who may attend only certain activities or whose involvement is restricted to special times of the year, such as Christmas or Easter.

The principal activities in which the Brazilian CEBs, like those elsewhere, engage are many and varied. Some focus on Bible study and reflection, some on mass or sacrament preparation; others (for example, women's and mothers' groups) coalesce around specific life interests. Still others focus squarely on political activities designed to raise consciousness or to improve the quality of life in the local area. What all share, however, is a central religious character combined with a willingness to engage, at some level, in this-worldly undertakings designed to enhance the quality of life in Brazilian society.

Theoretical perspectives on religion and social change

This study of the CEB phenomenon offers a detailed portrait of base-community structure and organization in Brazil. More important, though, it attempts to analyze the CEBs' role in helping to reshape the basic contours of Brazilian society. Thus, it has as its principal subject the relationship between religion and social change—or, to be more precise, the way in which religious faith and religious organizations bring about gradual, or even revolutionary, transformations of existing social structure.

Most certainly, the way in which religious belief and practice have affected this-worldly arrangements generally, especially in developing countries such as Brazil, has been a source of considerable debate. For developmentalists of a structural-functionalist bent, who see economic and sociopolitical change along Western lines as a quasi-inevitability, religion is largely viewed as an impediment to progress. Faith-related matters, along with other aspects of traditional culture, are seen by developmentalists, such as W. W. Rostow, for example, as standing in the way of the emergence of appropriate attitudes and institutions whose presence is required to ensure the maximization of modernizing activity.[1]

Somewhat interesting, as well, the developmentalists—most of whom accept and uphold capitalism as the solution to Third World problems—have found an ally in Marxism where their view of religious faith is concerned. Marx himself spoke disparagingly of religion, believing it to play a considerable role in the capitalist order by blinding proletarians to the servitude they endured at the hands of the dominant class. Taking Ludwig Feuerbach, Bruno Bauer, and others to task, moreover, he argued that religion was so tightly bound to the imperatives of domination that it could not be banished from this earth by an act of will. Rather, it would disappear only upon the displacement of capitalism.[2]

Those who have followed in Marx's wake are more divided in their perception of religion's worldly role. Dependency theorists, who see a world division of labor characterized by dominant core and subordinate peripheral nations, tend to share Marx's conception of religion as a tool of oppression. On the one hand, it may be used by dominant countries to ensure docility among the populations of those that are subordinate. On the other hand, for adherents of the "dual economy" view, religion is a remnant of an anterior mode of production that, while assuming less and less importance in the "modern" economic sector, may be used by elites to oppress subordinate classes in the "traditional" sector.[3]

Other Marxists, including Antonio Gramsci and, more recently, Otto Maduro, have come to see the relationship between religion and social change in a much different light. In a departure from the Marxian formula, Gramsci, first of all, has argued that cultural superstructure—of which religion is a part—is not simply a reflection of material infrastructure at any given point. Rather, the two possess a reality unto themselves and are therefore potentially codetermining in the process of historical change. Though clearly antireligious in many respects, Gramsci thus concedes that religion, as it is interpreted and acted upon by individuals, represents a source of power within society—rivaling, in fact, the socialist option. True enough, he does argue that for much of its history, the European Catholic Church, in particular, has reinforced the structure of class domination insofar as it has unswervingly upheld a high degree of unity between the popular classes and its own intellectuals. Nevertheless, given that religion is socio-historically grounded, Gramsci leaves the door open to the possibility that Church intellectuals may someday serve the interests of the believing, subordinate classes—with revolutionary consequences.[4]

Maduro even more lucidly affirms a role for religion in the process of social change. In his view, the church is a relatively autonomous social institution that, because its membership is typically drawn from the full spectrum of life experience, is shaped by, and actively shapes, the wider dynamics of class struggle. Throughout history, Maduro notes—as does Gramsci—the agenda of the Catholic Church, in particular, has been directed by dominant classes. Nevertheless, during specific historical moments, especially when sensitivity to the need for change is high among Church elites—owing, for example, to alterations in religious teaching—the demands of subordinate classes may find a certain receptivity within the Church. When this occurs, the religious symbols of the institution may be redirected to the service of the poor in aid of their broader struggle for social justice.[5]

Outside of the developmentalist and Marxist traditions, the most comprehensive treatment of religion and social change appears in the work of Max Weber. For Weber, the premise that religion and religious faith could produce real consequences for the life of the planet was simply beyond question. Weber certainly agreed with Marx that religion is often an expression of class interest and can be used to justify and maintain the subordination of whole classes. Unlike Marx, however, he held that the sphere of religious life, though connected to the material world, can and often does evolve in accordance with its own logic and necessity. Moreover, it may react back on social structure, having a far-reaching effect on the life conduct of all social classes.[6]

Interpretations of the worldly impact of specific religious innovations such as the CEBs are rarer in the literature than considerations of religion and change in general. Much of the work that has appeared originates from within liberation theology—a school of religious thought that is implicitly, and sometimes explicitly, rooted in the scholarly work of Marx and Gramsci. Although liberationist writing is extremely diverse, most authors of the genre claim to employ a "see-judge-act" methodology as they attempt to understand and assess social, political, economic, and even religious oppression from the perspective of the suffering poor, and as they encourage the active participation of the Church and other individuals and organizations in the creation of a more just social order.[7]

Following this framework, liberationists have come to interpret the CEBs as nothing less than the leading edge of an entirely renovated future religious and, more important, social structure. Through the groups' evangelizing practices, liberationists assert, the CEBs are stimulating *conscientização* (political awakening) and action on the part of the lower classes and thus are helping to create an entirely new social order. Initially, the process of change begins as the CEBs take on local causes, such as lobbying for running water and better bus service. From these beginnings, the CEBs, according to the liberationist view, create small, democratic, activist miniature societies from which the seeds of a more Christian and caring society will be cast.[8]

This rather utopian view of the CEBs is not, however, shared by all who have written about them. Political scientists such as Daniel H. Levine and Mainwaring, for example, see the impact of the CEBs in far less dramatic terms.[9] For these and other observers, the this-worldly significance of the CEBs lies not in their ability to transform social structure directly. Rather, the groups are seen as more subtly contributing to change by forging a new involvement-oriented political self-concept among group members. This in turn, it is argued, may enhance the presence and voice of the poor within the traditionally elitist structure of Latin American society and thereby ultimately contribute to a more equitable system of political decision making where the interests of the lower classes are taken fully into account.

Concurring with the general tone of the latter body of CEB research, the findings of this study also point to the more subtle aspects of the groups and their this-worldly influence. Moreover, regarding the broader theoretical questions about the relationship between religion and social change in general, the study results offer little comfort to those who would uphold the rather negative developmentalist paradigm or the more revolutionary models of religious innovation suggested by Gramsci or Maduro. Rather, the portrait of the CEBs sketched here would appear to both support and best fit the mold of Weberian sociology.

Of direct relevance to an interpretation of the essence of the phenomenon, Weber has stressed two factors that concern the appearance and the sustenance of religious innovations such as the CEBs. On the one hand, Weber has written at length on the pervasiveness and power of organizations—especially religious organizations. The Roman Catholic Church, in fact, is offered by Weber as a classic example of the modern organizational form. On the other hand, he has stressed the importance of specific types of religious actors and their success in encouraging the adoption of new forms of religious practice within society. Quite often, Weber has referred to the role of "prophets" in this regard, but he has also mentioned the vital function sometimes played by middle-class urban strata in promoting religious innovation. As I will demonstrate time and time again in this work, both the institutional presence of the Catholic Church and the roles played by key religious actors are vital components in CEB formation and activation.

In addition to providing these insights, Weber's now-famous work on the economic, social, and political consequences of the Protestant sects of Western Europe and America speaks directly to any investigation of the CEBs' social and political impact. Although Weber did not see Roman

Catholicism as particularly conducive to innovation, and although the CEBs are definitely not sects, they have, I will argue, stimulated new forms of religious thinking and, consequently, this-worldly involvement. Thus, though they may indeed be revolutionary, as the liberationist literature maintains, the CEBs can be seen, following Weber, as seeking to change the world more gradually—first and foremost by changing the way it is conceived in the minds of group members.

An overview of the CEB phenomenon in Brazil

Before proceeding to an examination of what indeed the CEBs are and of the various ways in which they attempt to transform Brazilian society, it is important first to locate the groups both conceptually and geographically. This is a far more difficult task than one might think, in spite of the confidence with which many authors have undertaken it.

Even simply defining a CEB is difficult. Officially, and for the purposes of this study, a *comunidade eclesial de base* is defined by breaking the term into its constituents. Thus, CEBs are *communities* because they consist of people who live in proximity to one another and have the same daily concerns. They are *ecclesial* because they are formed of people who are part of the Church and share the Catholic faith. And finally, they are of the *base* because they are formed primarily of people at the base of the Church, that is, the laity.[10] Another, less formal interpretation, and one that is also verified by this study, is provided by Mariano Baraglia, who defines a CEB as any group that meets on a regular basis to deepen its members' knowledge of the gospel, stimulate reflection and action on community needs, share victories and downfalls in the celebration of the Eucharist, and evangelize.[11]

Nevertheless, as Levine and Ivo Follmann have suggested, even rather elementary definitions such as these are subject to bitter dispute among interested parties and observers, especially those with particular ideological agendas.[12] Azevedo, for example, points out considerable variation in the way in which the terms employed to describe the CEBs are interpreted in the literature.[13] Questions arise about whether as communities, the CEBs replace or operate synthetically within the community exemplified by the parish. Not all agree, furthermore, that CEB members must be Catholics. Finally, there is considerable disagreement about what constitutes the "base." Many feel the base includes only those at the bottom of society— the poor—whereas others believe it includes all those with an interest in the liberating powers that the CEBs supposedly offer.

Similar disagreements arise over the types of activities in which the CEBs should properly be engaged.[14] Liberation theologians, for instance, suggest that only those groups participating in political action in defense of the lower classes can be considered bona fide CEBs. Others take a less stringent line and include groups that are on their way to becoming politically involved, and still others insist that even the most devotional groups can be CEBs so long as they consider themselves as such.

Where quantitative and geographical aspects of the CEB presence in Brazil are concerned, much more confusion reigns. To begin with, no one is quite sure about how many CEBs are actually in operation at any one time. At the national level exact figures are simply not available, although within individual dioceses some data on CEB numbers have been recorded. Even here, however, figures are less than reliable. For one thing, the collection of CEB data is wholly dependent upon the goodwill and ability of local pastors to gather information and pass it along to the local curia. In addition, because the CEBs are rather transitory, numbers may change dramatically from month to month and year to year. Another difficulty involves the definitional problem mentioned earlier: In effect, the local clergy must decide which groups should be included as CEBs and which should not. Quite often, values play a role in this assessment. Those pastors who strongly encourage the CEBs may overreport, believing that groups will become CEBs even if they are not now. Overreportage has also been known to occur when there is great pressure to show results on the CEB formation front. This is especially true in dioceses such as São Paulo, where CEB activation has received a high priority in official pastoral plans. Finally, there may be a tendency for clergy to deny the existence of CEBs when their presence is viewed with suspicion or disdain.

Rough estimates of CEB strength in Brazil do, of course, exist. Some of the earliest numbers were offered by the Centro de Estatística Religiosa e Investigações Sociais (CERIS), which in 1974 estimated that there were 40,000 groups operating in Brazil. In 1980 this estimate was raised by CERIS to 80,000.

Given the kinds of difficulties mentioned above, these numbers are still likely to be based as much on imagination as on statistical calculation. Nevertheless, because CERIS is affiliated with the Church, the figures have gained a certain credibility and are freely cited by numerous authors— with or without reference to their origin. Barreiro, for example, in his 1977 study of the CEBs referred to the 1974 CERIS estimate of 40,000.[15] Some studies done after 1980, including those of Betto, Irmão Michel, and Thomas G. Sanders, appear to have used the later CERIS number of 80,000.[16]

Other authors have applied other numbers to the CEB phenomenon, without apparent reference to the CERIS accounting. Writing in 1980 and 1982, Gottfried Deelen and Bruneau, respectively, suggested a figure of 50,000, while Pedro Oliveira, in a 1981 article, referred to some 60,000, far less than the 1980 CERIS figure. At the other end of the scale, more recent estimates have gone much higher than the 1980 CERIS count. Whereas some authors, such as Baldissera, have stuck with the 80,000 figure, the Catholic bishop Amaury Castanho has mentioned 100,000,[17] and press reports frequently talk about 150,000.[18]

Even greater variation is encountered in estimates of the number of people involved in the CEBs. Most of these are derived simply by multiplying estimates of group size by estimates of group numbers. Betto, for instance, taking an average of 20 to 30 members in 60,000 to 80,000 groups, claims there are at least two million Brazilians involved in the CEBs.[19] Clodovis Boff and Leonardo Boff cite double this number,[20] and Edward Cleary suggests that only about one million regularly attend CEB functions.[21] It should be pointed out here, however, that even if one accepts the numbers being used for estimating, such calculations are still likely flawed. This is because authors often fail to acknowledge that many CEB participants aren't "members" at all. In some cases, people simply take advantage of a group's geographical proximity to attend *some* religious services on a regular basis. Although, consequently, two or perhaps three million Brazilians may participate in the CEBs, the *level* at which they do so may disqualify many from actual CEB membership.

In addition to broad disagreement about definitional and quantitative aspects of the CEB presence in Brazil, there is also considerable difference of opinion about where the CEBs are physically situated. Historically, the conventional wisdom has suggested that the groups flourish primarily in the northeast of the country, with somewhat smaller numbers in the western, eastern, and southern regions.

To some extent, the perception of the CEBs as a regionally based phenomenon can be traced to studies conducted in 1973 and 1977 by Afonso Gregory and by Pedro Demo and Elizeu F. Calsing, respectively. The former study involved an examination of 43 CEBs; the latter, which was conducted for the National Conference of Brazilian Bishops (CNBB), sampled 101 groups from all parts of Brazil.[22] In both cases, most of the groups examined were situated in the northeastern region, with about one-third in the south and another quarter in the east. The central-western region accounted for only a small percentage of the samples.

Both Gregory and Demo and Calsing clearly cautioned that their samples were not representative. The groups under investigation were simply those that had responded to a national call for information about group characteristics and activities. Nevertheless, this work has, since its first appearance, more than occasionally been cited as evidence of CEB distribution patterns in Brazil.

Subsequent research, however, shows a more balanced proportioning of the CEB population throughout the country. In one study, informally conducted by the liberationist Clodovis Boff at a recent national CEB encounter at Trindade, Goiás, the CEBs were found to be present in the vast majority of dioceses in every region of the country.[23] A 4,200-respondent national survey of politico-religious attitudes and behavior conducted by the Instituto Universitário de Pesquisas do Rio de Janeiro (IUPERJ) similarly pointed to a more even geographical distribution of CEBs and other lay groups in Brazil.[24] For example, although 43 percent of all respondents in the study lived in northeastern states, the northeast accounted for only 39.7 percent of those claiming membership in church-affiliated associations. The southern region was similarly underrepresented, whereas the western and eastern regions had a disproportionately greater number of people claiming participation in Church groups. The results of an earlier study, conducted by Bruneau, support the overall trends identified by both Boff and the IUPERJ study.[25] Bruneau surveyed approximately 2,000 respondents in six dioceses throughout Brazil. He found participation in lay groups, including CEBs, to be highest in the western region, at about 15 percent, and lowest in the northeast, at 10 percent, with the southern region in between. More important, he discovered that a significant proportion of lay-group participants in all regions were involved in CEB-like activities. This ranged from a low of 66 percent in the south to a high of 85 percent in the central-west.

As for the CEBs' urban/rural situation, the conventional wisdom has suggested that most groups are found either in rural areas or on the periphery of Brazil's larger cities. The rationale for this perspective seems to be that such areas, which are home to the poor, provide extremely fertile ground for CEB formation and activation.

Few authors, however, offer more than speculative claims about the precise urban/rural ratio of the Brazilian CEBs. Such claims, moreover, are all too often accepted uncritically as established fact. Oliveira, for instance, relates that during an informal conversation with a colleague, he suggested that about two-thirds of all CEBs in Brazil were rural-based. To his dismay, this figure was later cited in a report and attributed to "research" conducted by him.[26]

What few statistically based estimates of the urban/rural dimension of the CEB phenomenon exist are seldom helpful. In the Demo-Calsing study cited earlier, for example, about 54 percent of all the CEBs were in rural areas. Seventeen percent were in urban areas, and 11 percent were on the periphery of metropolitan areas. Nineteen percent of the groups were listed as being of "unspecified" origin. Yet, virtually all of these "unspecified" groups were situated in the south. Because the south is the most urbanized region of Brazil, there is a strong likelihood that many of these CEBs were urban or suburban. Their inclusion in these categories, consequently, would certainly have increased the low proportions noted for these areas.

Contradicting the Demo-Calsing report, Gregory's figures show a predominance of urban-based CEBs. Only 5 percent of the 43 CEBs he examined were of unspecified origin, and only 30 percent were rural. The majority, some 65 percent, were situated in peripheral areas and, to a lesser extent, in urban districts proper. A less methodologically rigid study undertaken by Oliveira in 1981 confirmed Gregory's findings.[27] At the 1981 national CEB encounter at Itaici, Oliveira found that 62 percent of the CEBs in attendance were from urban areas. Twenty-four percent were from rural areas, and 3 percent of unspecified origin.

Conclusion

This study can offer little in the way of clarifying issues involving the quantitative and geographical aspects of the CEB phenomenon in Brazil. The present confusion in this area can be resolved only through the undertaking of a comprehensive, institutionally organized national inventory.

However, the study can and does have a good deal to say about the CEBs in many other fundamental respects. Specifically, it addresses what the groups are, what they do, and what they have managed to accomplish in the social and political spheres.

The investigation of these topics will proceed through a number of stages. In chapter 1, the origins of the CEBs in Brazil are examined in light of developments in both religion and politics since 1950. Chapter 2 discusses the birth and the scope of the CEB phenomenon in the archdiocese of São Paulo, where the primary research for the study was completed.

In chapters 3 and 4, group activities and organization are examined; particular emphasis is placed on the role of the institutional Church and the ways in which linkages with the Church have affected CEB formation and activation. In chapter 5, the social dimensions of the CEBs are dealt with; along with factors such as age and gender, the importance of social class is discussed and, in particular, the role that class has played in defining the limits of CEB action. Chapter 6 discusses the various organizational and orientational aspects of group life, mentioned earlier in more synthetic form, through a detailed examination of the day-to-day existence of two CEBs operating in different geographical and social settings. In chapters 7 and 8, the focus shifts to the more advanced and politically involved CEBs and the ways in which they effect social change; also examined in these chapters are the problems these more active groups have met and continue to encounter along the path to social justice. The book concludes with a discussion of where the CEBs and the Brazilian Church in general may be heading in the years to come.

1
The Origins of Church Innovation
∎

The vision of millions of ordinary Catholics seeking to express their faith in a new way and working together to solve real social problems through groups such as the CEBs is perhaps not easily accepted by those familiar with the long history of the Church in Latin America. For many, the question naturally arises of how groups of such obvious social and political potential could possibly arise from within what has traditionally been a rather conservative institution.

In actuality, the CEBs' appearance in Brazil and elsewhere in the region must be seen in the context of a major transformation in Church thinking and action occurring over a number of years. The Church in Latin America today is simply no longer as tightly bound to the status quo of society and politics as it once was.

For much of its long history, the Latin American Church had sought to defend its institutional interests and integrity by working hand in hand with governing elites—perpetuating, in effect, an oppressive social structure oriented toward the accumulation of great wealth among the few at the expense of an impoverished majority. Since at least 1950, however, from Chile to the countries of Central America, and even to Mexico, the Church has moved ever closer to the concerns of the socially disadvantaged and away from the concerns of those who hold power and privilege. In direct confrontation with the dominant classes of the region, the Church has encouraged social change through both words and action. Albeit to varying extents and degrees of enthusiasm, the national Churches of Latin America have, in unprecedented fashion, spoken out against injustice and encouraged the mobilization of the faithful at all institutional levels. Some Church members in countries such as Nicaragua and El Salvador have even resorted to violence in pursuit of their Church's revolutionary goals.

This change did not occur, of course, in a vacuum. Although in unequal measure and disparate combination—depending on the country in question—a host of both secular and religious factors formed the backdrop for the emergence of a "new" Church in Latin America after the close of World War II.[1] In one respect, Church change was a reaction to the crisis of modernization in the region and to the social ill effects of rapid industrialization and urbanization. In addition, a series of coups orchestrated by the military in several countries of the region after 1960, and the resultant rise of several politically and socially repressive bureaucratic-authoritarian states, demanded at least some response from an institution whose own members were often victimized. Finally, Church change was enhanced by the Church's own new social teaching emerging in the wake of the Second Vatican Council (1962–65). The Latin American bishops' meeting at Medellín, Colombia, was also critical in this regard. It was here, in fact, that the term which has come to symbolize the new direction of the Latin American Church—the "preferential option for the poor"—was coined.

Origins of the "preferential option for the poor" in Brazil

The dramatic process of change within the Latin American Church is perhaps seen most clearly in Brazil. Except for a relatively brief 40-year span following the proclamation of the Republic in 1889—a period during which Church and State were formally separated—the Brazilian Church had been strongly allied with governing authority for much of Brazil's history.[2] During the period of the Monarchy (1500–1889), this alliance was largely a function of the Church's dependency on the State for its institutional maintenance. Later, during the years of the Vargas dictatorship (1930–45), Church and regime were closely tied by an exchange-of-favor mechanism designed to secure their respective organizational goals. Upon the dissolution of Getúlio Vargas's Estado Novo (new state) in 1945 and the rise of liberal democracy in Brazil, however, the Church began to move off in a new direction, adopting a more confrontational stance with governing authority and taking the cause of the poor as its own—constructing, in other words, its own indigenous version of the "option for the poor" ultimately called for at the 1968 Latin American bishops' meeting at Medellín.

As it is applied here, the term "option for the poor" may be ambiguous and confusing. Historically, it would seem that the Roman Catholic

Church, whether within or outside Brazil, has always been the church of the poor, fulfilling their religious needs and dispensing charity when necessary. In Brazil, however, the Church is speaking not of caring for the poor in a material or spiritual sense, as it has traditionally done, but of adopting the cause of the poor, and of attacking the economic and political system that ostensibly perpetuates their poverty. The following quote from a 1983 Church document might best describe this new ideological position.

> An authentic evangelical commitment, such as that of Christ, is above all a commitment to those most in need; the Church in Brazil stresses the position taken at Puebla by the Latin American bishops to exercise its full evangelizing mission in light of a clear and prophetic preferential option for the poor, for the purpose of their total liberation.
>
> The preferential option for the poor is a clear commitment, unequivocal and evangelically inviolable, with the concrete cause of the impoverished in Brazilian society.[3]

The adoption of this commitment, which has established the Brazilian Catholic Church as one of the most politically progressive in Latin America, is of no minor consequence, considering the size and scope of the institution. With 242 ecclesiastical divisions, over 6,000 parishes, 355 bishops, 12,500 priests, and nearly 40,000 men and women religious, it is the second largest national Church in the world.[4] Moreover, it presides, in religious matters at least, over the world's largest and most populous Catholic country. Of the 140 million inhabitants who live within the nation's 8.5 million square kilometers, nearly 90 percent list their principal faith as Roman Catholic.[5]

As in Latin America generally, the changes that this formidable institution has undergone since 1950 cannot be seen in isolation. The move toward social justice coincided with several key events occurring over a 30-year span.

During the 1950s, to begin with, Brazil witnessed a tremendous shift in population from the countryside to the city, which resulted in considerable social upheaval. This shift was partly due to the lure of rapidly developing industry (especially in southeastern Brazil), but was also attributable to the rationalization of agricultural production, which increasingly spelled the end of feudal relations between landholders and peasants, and which "liberated" rural workers by the thousands. Many of those who left the land for Brazil's larger centers soon found themselves living in sprawling suburban neighborhoods, with no access to basic services and little chance of obtaining secure, well-remunerated employment. Those who remained on the land, either to work as day laborers or to secure a plot of their own, became increasingly militant, forming or joining one of the growing number of representative organizations in opposition to the powerful landlords.[6]

After 1964, Brazil was also subject to upheaval on the political front. In that year, Brazil's military seized power from the civilian president, João Goulart, as part of a bold move designed to protect the nation against what it saw as rampant corruption, communist infiltration, and imminent economic collapse. Until it eventually began to relax its grip on the nation in the late 1970s (the government was not returned to civilian hands until 1985), the new regime was essentially guided by an overwhelming concern with "national security." Its primary goals were to strengthen the presence of the armed forces throughout Brazilian territory, to modernize the country's political structure, and to foster rapid economic growth. These were to be achieved within the context of what is best described as a bureaucratic-authoritarian state, in which political, economic, and military planning were highly centralized. Opposition to the regime was severely repressed through media censorship and the imprisonment or exile of political dissidents. Moreover, although certain democratic institutions were formally maintained, opportunities for popular participation were curtailed through the passing of a series of constitutional amendments known as Institutional Acts.[7]

Another significant development coinciding with the rise of the "new" Church in Brazil originated in the cupola of Catholicism itself, in the form of radical new religious teaching. First there was the release of the final document of Vatican II, *Gaudium et Spes* (1965), which, in its affirmation of the validity of this-worldly concerns and its call for social justice, signaled a dramatic change in ecclesiastical thinking. This was followed some three years later, after their 1968 Medellín meetings, by the Latin American bishops' assessment and condemnation of regional poverty and oppression. Together, these documents from Vatican II and Medellín were viewed with great interest in Brazil, insofar as they seemed to speak directly to the social and political problems plaguing the country.[8]

In summary then, it should be clear that the Brazilian Church's "option for the poor" evolved alongside some dramatic changes in the social, political, and religious life of the nation. It did not just appear overnight, but took shape gradually over nearly three decades. Indeed, in the beginning, the Church's move down the path of social-justice concerns was, without question, tentative and sporadic.

Perhaps the earliest development signaling a new direction in the Church was the publication, in 1950, of Dom Inocêncio Engelke's "Conosco, sem nós, ou contra nós, se fará a reforma rural" (With us, without us, or against us, rural reform will be made).[9] The bishop's statement was, in fact, a landmark document, calling for extensive agrarian reform in Brazil. The early 1950s also witnessed the strengthening of specialized urban and rural Catholic Action groups in Brazil, such as the Juventude Operária Católica (Working-Class Catholic Youth), the Juventude Universitária Católica (University Catholic Youth), the Juventude Agrária Católica (Agrarian Catholic Youth), and the Juventude Estudantil Católica (Student Catholic Youth).[10] These and other similar groups sought to promote change in Brazil on a broad basis by encouraging those in their respective milieus to be aware of the social problems around them.

Another important occurrence during this period was the formation of the National Conference of Brazilian Bishops (CNBB) in 1952. Founded by a core of social progressives within the episcopate, this organization was instrumental in effecting change along numerous fronts. To begin with, it provided growing space in the institutional Church for the various specialized Catholic Action groups mentioned above. Second, stimulated by Bishop Eugenio Sales's experiment with radio schools in Natal in 1958, the CNBB established a rural education network aimed at promoting both literacy and social awareness among the northeastern peasantry.[11] After 1961, the program, which was termed the Basic Education Movement (MEB), was expanded to other parts of Brazil with the aid of government funding. Third, by 1959 the CNBB had become involved in rural unionization, helping peasants to organize in a number of predominantly agrarian states.[12] Finally, statements released by the CNBB and its regional divisions helped to promote awareness of and offer solutions to the problems affecting the Brazilian lower classes. In 1956, for example, northeastern bishops denounced rural poverty in a statement entitled "Declaração de Campina Grande" (Campina Grande declaration). Furthermore, in 1962 the CNBB as a whole published its first joint plan, the *Plano de emergência* (plan of emergency), through which it sought to define priorities for future pastoral action in the social and political arenas.[13]

This momentum established by certain progressive elements within the laity and the upper ranks of the hierarchy came to an abrupt halt, however, with the military coup of 1964. In their attempts to control "subversion," the ruling generals introduced several repressive measures that rendered impossible much of the work the Church had begun in the social-justice area. To make matters worse, the repression exacerbated a split within the Church between more progressive and more conservative clergy—many of whom, in fact, supported the takeover.[14] Eventually, though, the institution did close ranks in opposition to the regime and moved once again, this time more united than ever, to commit itself to the cause of the oppressed lower classes.

Evidence of the regeneration of the Brazilian Catholic Church as a force defending the interests of the socially disadvantaged in Brazil is clearly present in the various documents published by the CNBB and its regional divisions after 1970. In 1973, the northeastern bishops' "Eu ouvi os clamores do meu povo" (I have heard the cry of my people) expressed solidarity with the lower classes in no uncertain terms. A similar release, "Marginalização de um povo" (Marginalization of a people), was also published that year by bishops from the central-west of Brazil.

After 1975, a number of other important documents began to appear at the national level. Principal among these were *Comunicação pastoral ao povo de Deus* (Pastoral message to the people of God) (1976), *Exigências Cristãs de uma ordem política* (Christian requirements for a political order) (1977), and *Subsídios para uma política social* (Aids for a social policy) (1979).[15] Even after a period of liberalization (*abertura*) that was initiated by the military and lasted through the late 1970s and early 1980s, the CNBB continued to promote the cause of the poor through such documents as *Reflexão Cristã sobre a conjuntura política* (1981; Christian reflection on the political situation) and *Solo urbano e ação pastoral* (1982; Urban land and pastoral action).[16]

Through the CNBB, the Church has worked as well to establish national programs in defense of human rights. In 1973, the Conselho Indigenísta Missionário (Native Missionary Council) was formed to help Brazil's aboriginal peoples protect themselves from arbitrary abuses. Some two years later, the CNBB created the Comissão Pastoral de Terra (Pastoral Land Commission), which has since endeavored to defend the rights of small landholders in Brazil. In addition to these programs, the CNBB has encouraged the formation of human-rights defense groups at all ecclesiastical levels within the Church and, perhaps most important, has stalwartly supported the development of popular organizations such as the CEBs.[17]

Interpretations of Church innovation since 1950

Because of the duration of the process, the complexity of secular and religious factors, and the multiplicity of players involved, a number of theories have naturally arisen that attempt to account for Church change since 1950. In her work, Vanilda Paiva has discussed seven of these, formulated by authors both inside and outside Brazil.[18] Here, however, only three of the broader paradigms will be discussed—namely, the institutional, grass-roots, and intermediate approaches.

The earliest and now longest standing of these models is the institutional perspective. In essence, explanations of this genre hold that the "option for the poor" is best understood as an elite-generated strategy—one designed to deal with a variety of religious and secular pressures threatening the integrity and influence of the institutional Church.

Within the institutional school, one of the most straightforward accounts of Church change is provided by Roberto Romano.[19] Basically, he sees recent alterations in Church thinking and action as a mechanism developed to maintain continued Catholic hegemony over a population whose allegiance is increasingly threatened by the prevailing social, economic, and political tensions. Through the creation and implementation of a Catholic social-justice program, claims Romano, the Church has simply moved to renovate its own timeworn instruments of domination in order to retain its historic constituency and thus ensure institutional salvation.

Another, somewhat more sophisticated view of Church change from the institutional perspective is offered by Ivan Vallier.[20] He has argued that within various Latin American Churches, including Brazil's, recent modifications—such as increased centralization, the development of a lay apostolate, and the adoption of a social ideology relevant to the masses—were initiated by the upper hierarchy as part of a calculated response to three specific challenges. These were (1) the rise of new value movements in Latin America, such as Protestantism, socialism, and Afro-American spiritism; (2) the need for increased levels of institutional integration to keep pace with a modernizing milieu; and (3) the pressure emanating from international Catholicism for the Latin American Church to awaken to its social responsibilities.

In a similar fashion, Ralph Della Cava has interpreted institutional and ideological transformation in the Church as an attempt to solve a grave crisis that began to beset it after 1950.[21] In Brazil, he claims, this crisis was distinguished by two basic features. The first of these was the collapse of the Church's leadership structure following the death of the powerful and influential Cardinal Sebastião Leme. The second and perhaps more serious dilemma facing the Church was the erosion of its religious monopoly, brought about by factors such as (1) the endemic lack of clergy in Brazil, made especially acute by a rapidly expanding population; (2) a persistently low level of religiosity among the nominally Catholic masses; and (3) the growth of Protestantism and certain popular movements (especially on the political left) that found fertile soil for development in the ever-worsening living conditions of the lower classes.

One of the more completely developed explanations of the institutional genre, finally, is offered by Bruneau.[22] At base, Bruneau's interpretation is essentially consonant with arguments put forth by Romano, Vallier, and Della Cava, insofar as it suggests that it was clearly the hierarchy that led the Church down the social-justice path in Brazil and elsewhere in Latin America. What distinguishes his approach from the others, though, is that it attempts to understand Church action since 1950 as more than simply a calculated response to particular social and religious challenges or threats.

Historically, claims Bruneau, the goal of the Catholic Church has been influence, which it seeks so that it can fulfill its worldly mission of salvation. In Brazil, until recently, the Church sought to implement this goal by forging an institutional alliance with the State. During the 1950s, however, confronted by both the grim reality of the emerging social situation in Brazil and imminent threats to the survival of the institution, the upper hierarchy of the Church began to reorient its operational method, opting for an independent strategy of "pre-influence." This strategy, claims Bruneau, advocates that society as a whole should be transformed—not as an end in itself, but to make religious influence inherently meaningful to ordinary Brazilians at some point in the future. Thus, the "option for the poor" emerged, Bruneau asserts, "not due to short-run strategies, but in pursuit of long-run visions of society which are based in theology."[23]

One of the most important factors in the eventual refinement of the "option"—aside from the influence of important Church documents released in the progressive aftermath of Vatican II—adds Bruneau, was the 1964 coup and military takeover of the Brazilian government. Initially welcomed by a good portion of the hierarchy (for putting an end to supposed communist subversion), the arbitrary arrest and torture of more radical religious individuals became, over time, a focal point of conflict between the military government and a growing number of priests, nuns, and bishops. Such conflict, in turn, not only challenged the clergy to come forward en bloc in aid of their Church, but also helped the institution to clarify and underline the differences between its own newfound goals of social justice and the "national security" objectives of the State.

Although this approach and others of the institutional viewpoint are now widely accepted by students of the Church, they have certainly not escaped criticism. In their assessment of recent Church history, one group of authors, for instance, have taken Bruneau and others to task for downplaying the broader societal context and, in particular, the actions of the lower classes themselves in the formation of the Brazilian Church's "option for the poor." These commentators—the bulk of whom are liberation theologians—constitute what might best be referred to as the grass-roots school.

In contrast to the institutional theorists, who draw heavily on a Weberian conception of religious and organizational transition, advocates of the liberationist grass-roots approach largely prefer a modified Marxian interpretation of social change. Consequently, they place less emphasis on the role of leadership, or official doctrine—such as that emerging from Vatican II or Medellín—in the development of the "option," focusing instead on the prophetic role of the dominated classes in effecting religious transformation. Enrique Dussel, for example, has spoken of the Church's new social mission in Latin America as emanating not from the superstructure of Catholicism but from a "people-rooted Christianity that has been gestating . . . over the past twenty-five years."[24] This "people-rooted" style of faith, explains fellow liberationist Gustavo Gutierrez, originates with the social irruption, or "breaking in," of the oppressed masses in the region, who are making their presence felt through concrete struggles for liberation from political and economic oppression. In time, Gutierrez insists, this "shift from absence to presence" within the societal sphere also takes place within the Church. "There too," he observes, "the poor are increasingly getting across [to the hierarchy] their right to live their faith."[25] Similarly, claims Leonardo Boff, as part of a broad "strategy to win more power and autonomy in the face of the domination from which they are suffering," the poor have successfully managed to appeal to their Church for assistance.[26]

Albeit in somewhat more complex fashion, the Venezuelan liberationist Maduro also sees Church change as linked to class conflict.[27] For Maduro, the Church, in Brazil and Latin America generally, is a relatively autonomous institution in society. As such, it is, on the one hand, shaped by larger societal processes. As the Church embraces both dominant and subordinate class actors, it contains the full dynamics of class struggle. On the other hand, it can actively shape social processes, depending on the orientation of the constituencies that control the institution at any given historical moment. Traditionally, claims Maduro, the Church, thus defined, has been controlled by those with money and power. In response to the historic suppression of the lower classes' economic and political aspirations, however—a situation exacerbated by the installation of a string of repressive military dictatorships throughout the region after 1960—the poor have, in recent years, turned steadily to the Church as one place where they can freely express their opposition to the structures of domination. In doing so, they have, in effect, moved to break down elitist control within the Church and push the institution to speak out more clearly on their behalf. Two factors have helped facilitate this popular "takeover." To begin with, the adoption of the cause of the poor by the Church was made more attractive after 1965 by the new thinking expressed in the documents of Vatican II and Medellín; and second, the growing repression of the Church in many countries caused a rift between the Church and the traditional dominant classes, thus forcing the leadership of the institution to rethink its support of the status quo.

Between the institutional and grass-roots perspectives, there is, finally, what might be called an intermediate approach. In examining the Brazilian case, authors of this persuasion, including Lima, Mainwaring, and Adriance, attempt to take a middle road by broadening the bases of input into the "option" while allowing for at least some measure of hierarchical control over its fate.[28]

Lima, in his account of Church change in Brazil after 1950, focuses on the interplay between two distinct constituencies located at the lower and upper levels of the Church—the laity involved in Catholic Action, and the progressive episcopate. Catholic Action, for its part, worked at the base of the Church in well-defined groups (workers, peasants, students, etc.) to directly transform unjust social structures, thus pushing the institution ever leftward. The progressive episcopate fulfilled a similar role at the upper levels of the Church but was also instrumental in legitimating and expanding the work done at the grass roots by Catholic Action. In pursuing its goals, this minority within the upper hierarchy, Lima adds, was not merely responding to threats, as some in the institutional camp have held; nor were the progressive bishops reacting to the emergence of progressive social teaching alone. Rather, they were strongly influenced by the progressive social movements already active in Brazil and, more specifically, by the growing core of progressive Catholic laity involved in the transformation process.

Mainwaring agrees with Lima's recognition of both elite and lay factors in his examination of Church change. He upholds the powerful role of the hierarchy in initiating and sustaining change—a principal tenet of the institutional approach. But at the same time, he criticizes Bruneau and others for underestimating the extent to which alterations in episcopal thinking and action—alterations that led to the adoption of the "option for the poor"—were conditioned by initiatives undertaken at the base of the institution. The recent actions of the Church, claims Mainwaring, cannot thus be seen simply as part of a unidimensional, elite-generated strategy designed to effect institutional salvation. On the contrary, Church change in Brazil has evolved rather dialectically as a product of elite-lay interaction.

The work of Adriance, finally, maintains a compatibility with that of both Lima and Mainwaring while at the same time offering unique insights into the process of institutional transformation. To a considerable extent, Adriance confirms Lima's and Mainwaring's assertions about the influence of lay activists on Church thinking and action after 1950. But she also holds, in keeping with the institutional approach, that the Church's move toward social justice was, in fact, mediated by the hierarchy—often with self-serving motives. In a novel departure, however, Adriance asserts that institutional influence over the course of the "option for the poor" has increasingly come to be threatened by popular influence, which has, to this point, pushed and expanded the "option" in ways unanticipated by its original architects.

As for the ultimate utility of these various models within each of the institutional, grass-roots, and intermediate approaches, certainly all offer at least some valid insights regarding Church change. In the Brazil of the 1950s and early 1960s, there did exist numerous secular and religious challenges to Church hegemony and institutional integrity with which Church leaders were likely forced to deal, as advocates of the institutional perspective have argued. At the other end of the scale, there can be little doubt that both Catholic Action and more popular forms of initiative in the social-justice sphere helped to forge new directions within the Church, as grass-roots and intermediate theorists have suggested.

But in evaluating each of the approaches posited here, what needs to be assessed is the actual contribution of all factors and influences to Church change, in light of available evidence. There is a particular problem with the grass-roots approach in this respect, because it offers little empirical substantiation to support its claims for a popular "takeover" of religious symbolism. To a lesser extent, the same is true of the intermediate approach. Although these authors do point to specific programs and activities undertaken by lay sectors such as Catholic Action, they still provide no way to effectively measure the influence such groups may have had on the leadership of the Church.

What can be more easily demonstrated empirically is the basic claim of the institutional approach that the process of change within the Church has been the result, in the final analysis, of a highly controlled and regulated elite strategy. Such a strategy is, in fact, revealed in documents outlining and justifying Church programs and priorities in the social-justice arena, and in the existence and day-to-day operation of specific Church initiatives (as outlined earlier in this chapter).

This evidence for the fundamental role of strategy does not negate the possibility that the hierarchy has been influenced by the actions of laypersons and religious individuals working at lower levels of the institution. It does speak strongly, however, to the question of who, finally, controls the direction of the Church within the realm of society and politics—namely, the bishops. Of that—and this is a point which intermediate and even grass-roots theorists are reluctant to dispute—there can be little doubt.

CEB activation and growth

Just as Church change in Brazil has been subject to intense scrutiny of late, so too has the ascension of the CEBs attracted much attention. Indeed, insofar as these groups represent the most innovative and pervasive form of this-worldly intervention on the part of the "new" Church, the CEBs' progress has been researched and chronicled with much zeal.

As one might expect, general interpretations of the CEB ascension are diverse, in effect mirroring existing arguments about the emergence of the "option for the poor." Thus, institutional theorists point to the CEBs as part of a strategy to enhance organizational strength and maintain influence in a changing world. Liberation theologians see the CEBs as evidence of a spontaneously emergent expression of the popular will and, consequently, as evidence supporting their view of change within the Church at large. Those in the middle tend to look at the CEBs as a product of more complicated interplay between hierarchy and base.

Yet, despite fundamental disagreements, there is considerable concordance among students of the CEBs regarding the specific social and political factors that facilitated the emergence and growth of the CEB phenomenon over the years. Moreover, though certainly not all agree about the degree of institutional interference in the CEBs' rise to prominence, few authors have ignored the role of the Church and its leaders in promoting the groups.

Concerning the initial appearance of the phenomenon, most authors will agree that it is extremely difficult to assign the status of "first CEB" to any one base community. Rather, the groups are viewed as having appeared sporadically, in various parts of the country, over a period of years around 1960. After that time, the CEBs are seen as proliferating freely and rapidly under diverse conditions.

According to most accounts, as well, the path to this success was initially cleared by lay-group activation stimulated during the 1950s by the various Catholic Action groups mentioned previously.[29] Later, it is argued, this initiative came to be legitimated and enhanced by the Second Vatican Council (1962–66), which called for the Church to move closer to the faithful, and for the faithful, in turn, to become more intensely involved in the promotion of social justice.

Further impetus for CEB formation is seen to have been provided by the 1968 meeting of Latin American bishops held at Medellín, Colombia. During this encounter, the episcopate soundly criticized existing Church structure as being out of touch with the reality of Latin America, and called for the hierarchy to focus its attention firmly on the plight of the disadvantaged classes in the region. As the best means for effecting both the revitalization of the Church as an institution and the liberation of the poor from economic and political oppression, the bishops cited the CEBs in particular. This call was welcomed with special enthusiasm in Brazil, it has been suggested, as a solution to the Church's relative institutional weakness (given the size of the country) and the deplorable conditions under which the vast majority of the population were forced to live.

Secular factors contributing to CEB development are traced primarily to the increasing economic and political repression felt in Brazil in the wake of the 1964 coup. In some ways, commentators maintain, the harsh measures adopted by the generals did have certain positive effects on Brazilian society. The Brazilian economy, for example, began to revive after nearly collapsing in the early years of the decade. By 1967, inflation had fallen and investor confidence had grown dramatically. In the years following, moreover, the economy grew at unprecedented annual rates over 10 percent, prompting many to speak of a Brazilian economic "miracle" in the making. But while the middle and upper classes benefited greatly from this upswing, the rewards frequently promised to the lower classes by the ruling military never, in fact, materialized. If anything, the poor actually became poorer during the boom years of the late 1960s and early 1970s. Between 1960 and 1977, for instance, the top 1 percent of the economically active population increased its share of the national income from 11.9 percent to 18.3 percent. The poorest half, by comparison, saw its share drop from 17.4 percent to a mere 13.1 percent.[30] To make matters worse, the situation of the average worker deteriorated still further after 1974. It was in this year that the Brazilian "miracle" began to go flat, as the economy faltered under the weight of soaring import bills (especially for crude oil) and a shrinking export market that was brought about by recession in the industrialized world. This, in turn, spelled higher inflation and growing unemployment in all economic sectors.

The economic hardship, borne primarily by the disadvantaged classes, provided a backdrop for increasing social unrest in Brazil in the years after the military coup. Unfortunately, however, the government had successfully managed to bring under its control virtually all vehicles of political expression, and the poor were thus left with few avenues of legitimate protest. The Church, to a considerable extent, stepped in to fill this void. In addition to creating a number of strategies and organizations in defense of human rights, to the poor and oppressed the Church offered the CEBs, which served as shelters from which the people could express their disenchantment with the political and economic status quo.

Conclusion

One inescapable conclusion can be drawn from the processes and analyses presented in this chapter: the emergence of the CEBs cannot be understood outside of the long and involved process of change occurring within both Brazilian Catholicism and Brazilian society generally since 1950. Students of the Church may debate the ultimate cause of Church innovations, including the CEBs, but they fundamentally agree about the degree and direction of change, and the nature of the basic social and religious contexts in which change has taken place.

Another subject on which there has been agreement—in some measure, at least—is the extent to which the CEBs, as instruments of social change, have been accompanied by the institutional Church throughout their history. The Church, for its part, has in fact insisted upon a strong role vis-à-vis the CEBs and has reaffirmed its close ties to the groups in count-less directives. As one 1983 CNBB document holds, the CEBs are "a strictly ecclesial phenomenon born in the breast of the institutional Church" and, as such, are required to maintain "a sincere and loyal connection between the community and its legitimate ministers, in a faithful adherence to the objectives of the Church, in a total opening-up to other communities, and to the great community of the universal Church."[31]

This propensity to very close CEB-institutional bonds distinguishes the Brazilian CEB movement from, say, that of Nicaragua, where the disjuncture between the activist laity and clergy and the upper hierarchy is well documented. It also goes a considerable distance in explaining the unique nature and thrust of the CEB phenomenon in Brazil, as will be demonstrated.

2
Innovation
in the
Archdiocese
of São Paulo
–

The importance of ecclesiastical accompaniment to the CEB phenomenon can be shown no more clearly than in the archdiocese of São Paulo. Here, as much as anywhere else in Brazil, the CEBs have received substantial encouragement and guidance. As a result, São Paulo today boasts the largest concentration of active groups in the country.

At the root of the local church's unwaivering sponsorship of the CEBs lies its firm commitment to social justice. Without question, São Paulo has shown a great deal of leadership in both its willingness and its skill in implementing the "preferential option for the poor" first articulated at the national level by the CNBB.

Socioeconomic characteristics

In some ways, the metropolitan São Paulo area would seem an unlikely venue for the "option" to take root in. It is, after all, a very large (16 million inhabitants) and relatively affluent center, with a solid economic base. With 11 percent of the nation's total population, São Paulo possesses approximately 16 percent of Brazil's 214,000 industrial establishments. These companies employ 29 percent of all industrial workers in the country, and produce more than one-fifth of the country's annual gross product.[1] In addition, salaries in São Paulo are among the best in Brazil, with per capita income approximately double the national figure.[2] Moreover, about 14 percent of São Paulo's work force earn in excess of five times the minimum monthly salary[3] as compared with only 7 percent of Brazilian wage earners generally.[4] São Paulo also possesses far fewer low-wage earners than does the nation on average. Whereas 22 percent of all declared wage earners in Brazil take home the minimum salary or less, only 10 percent of *Paulistanos* fall into this category.

In the midst of this seeming affluence, however, a number of serious social and economic problems exist that have made a commitment to the "option for the poor" both desirable and, to some extent, imperative for the local Church. To begin with, there have been chronic unemployment and inflation—problems that were recently exacerbated in the wake of a strong recession beginning in 1980.[5] Since that year, the rates for both have varied wildly from month to month in a way they would not from year to year in more developed countries. Unemployment ranges anywhere from 4 percent to 15 percent of the work force at any given time—depending on whose figures are cited.[6] As a result, during harder times, thousands of individuals are placed on the streets, where, due to the absence of any comprehensive welfare system, they join the already bloated ranks of itinerant street vendors and panhandlers jockeying for change. Inflation runs from 9 percent or 10 percent to as high as 30 percent per month. Moreover, despite periodic adjustments designed to protect low-income workers, salaries in São Paulo have all too seldom kept pace with the cost of living.[7]

The recession in São Paulo has also made a long-time problem of extreme social inequality even more severe. In spite of the apparent sophistication of the central regions of the city, over 70 percent of São Paulo's inhabitants live in poverty in squalid slums or self-constructed housing in areas surrounding the central core and covering three-quarters of the city's total domain.[8]

This peripheral zone is frequently overlooked by tourists and more affluent Brazilians, yet it has been growing at a phenomenal pace, bloated by a steady stream of job-seeking migrants from neighboring Minas Gerais and various other northeastern states.[9] During the 1960s, the southern and eastern peripheral zones were in fact growing at the fantastic annual rates of 11 percent and 15 percent, respectively. More recent figures show that they continue to expand at a rate of approximately 5 percent to 7 percent—twice the municipal average.[10]

The quality of life on the outskirts of São Paulo can be described only as precarious. Family incomes are extremely low, averaging at least three to four times less than those in more affluent areas of the city. The proportion of low-income families (those earning under five minimum salaries per month), moreover, is quite high. Whereas only about 21 percent of all resident families in the middle-class suburbs of Ibirapuera and Perdizes earn less than five minimum salaries, nearly two-thirds (64 percent) of families in the sprawling districts of Itaquera and Capela do Socorro subsist on this amount.[11]

Housing on the periphery is predominantly self-constructed and thus usually substandard, with little or no adherence to building codes or basic safety requirements.[12] Furthermore, the relatively high cost of building materials restricts the size of homes, resulting in crowded living conditions for most families. In the peripheral subdistrict of Brasilândia, for example, there are on average 3 persons per bedroom, compared with only 1.5 in other, more affluent areas such as Pinheiros.[13]

To make matters worse, there is an almost total lack of infrastructure in the area. Most suburban streets are unpaved, and though many areas are now served by electricity and running water, street lighting is frequently lacking.[14] Police protection is virtually nonexistent, and this, combined with poor lighting, has tended to aggravate an already soaring crime rate in many poor neighborhoods.[15] The majority of homes outside central São Paulo, moreover, are not connected to sewers. In most neighborhoods, raw sewage is simply allowed to run down drainage ditches and into the nearest stream. In the municipality's eastern districts, this problem is especially acute. In 1982, for example, only 14,000 of an estimated 300,000 households in the São Miguel administrative district were connected with the city's sewer system.[16]

Health and related care services, for their part, are all but absent. Hospitals and first-aid centers are usually situated in the more central, affluent areas of the city. The central core and surrounding neighborhoods, in fact, contain within their boundaries 44 percent of all the hospitals and treatment centers in São Paulo, serving only 16 percent of the city's total population. By contrast, the eastern districts, with 26 percent of the population, have but 6 percent of all such facilities.[17] The unequal distribution of health services shows dramatically in the infant mortality rate in these same two areas. In the center, the rate for 1983 was 29 deaths per 1,000 live births, whereas the rate for the poorer, eastern districts was considerably higher, at 51 deaths.[18]

Finally, transportation is extremely poor. São Paulo's transit system has consistently proven unable to provide the eight million commuters who use it daily with any degree of comfort, safety, or reliability. To further tilt the scales, having to locate on the periphery (because of the low land costs) invariably means being far from one's workplace. On average, transportation studies have shown, a worker spends some three to four hours each day traveling to and from his or her place of work.[19]

Implementation of an "option for the poor"

Effectively implementing an "option for the poor" designed to help the poor meet the challenge of living in a city like São Paulo has not been easy, especially with the size and scope of the local Church bureaucracy.[20] Before it was reorganized in early 1989, the archdiocese of São Paulo included all of the municipality of São Paulo (population 11 million) and several smaller townships that form part of the metropolitan region.[21] With a population of over 14 million, it was the largest ecclesiastical unit of its kind in the world. Territorially, São Paulo's 5,000-square-kilometer land area was divided into nine episcopal regions, which together contained some 53 sectors and 395 parishes. Serving the faithful were one archbishop, 10 auxiliary bishops (9 of which presided directly over the episcopal regions), approximately 450 secular priests, 700 priests in orders, and 3,500 men and women religious. In addition, within its boundaries, the archdiocese owned or controlled a number of religious institutions and properties. Along with church buildings and related structures, there were no less than 11 secular seminaries and 26 others belonging to various religious orders, five ecclesiastical study centers, an archive, 10 higher-learning institutes (including a major university, Pontifícia Universidade Católica), and dozens of *colégios* offering elementary- and secondary-school courses.

That an institution of this size functioned with any degree of efficiency in facilitating the traditional requirements of Roman Catholicism is quite an accomplishment. To have it turn its considerable weight in an entirely new and innovative direction—especially during a period of intense government repression—is truly remarkable. Yet, this is precisely what did occur after 1970 when the archdiocese of São Paulo chose to make its "preferential option for the poor."

Much of the credit for this transformation must go to one of the leading members of the CNBB and the longtime archbishop of São Paulo, Cardinal Paulo Evaristo Arns. This is not to say that the archdiocese was largely devoid of innovative activity before Arns's arrival. Certainly, the CEBs had existed there since at least the early 1960s. In addition, the former archbishop, Agnello Rossi, had already begun extremely important work in defense of the civil and human rights of political detainees, often held without charge in São Paulo's military jails. Nevertheless, in Arns's absence, the São Paulo Church could probably never have come to enjoy the reputation it has today as a staunch defender of the oppressed.

The first signs of Dom Paulo's deep commitment to social justice were clearly seen shortly after he assumed command of the archdiocese in 1970. It was during this time that he intensified earlier work, begun during his tenure as auxiliary bishop, in defense of hundreds of churchmen and laypersons arbitrarily detained by the military following the coup of 1964.

To bring the plight of these unfortunate men and women to light, Dom Paulo exhausted every means at his disposal. In 1972, he published and distributed a statement entitled "Testemunha de paz" (Testimony of peace), which condemned the use of torture in São Paulo's jails. This same concern was reiterated by Dom Paulo and his auxiliary bishops some three years later in a pamphlet called "Não oprimas teu irmão" (Do not oppress thy brother), published after the death of the imprisoned journalist Vladimir Herzog.[22] In addition to issuing these statements, Cardinal Arns made extensive use of the archdiocesan newspaper O São Paulo and radio station Nove de Julho to expose instances of injustice, met frequently with government officials on behalf of prisoners and their families, and made regular prison visits to console dozens of individuals who had suffered mental and physical abuse at the hands of their captors. Such efforts earned him the respect of world leaders including U.S. President Jimmy Carter, with whom Cardinal Arns had met on a number of occasions.[23]

Over the years, Cardinal Arns's association with political detainees also helped him to develop and clarify his role as defender of the oppressed generally in São Paulo. Dom Paulo recently wrote, "One day I confessed to myself, 'My God, I am becoming less the Archbishop of the city, and more the Archbishop of the prisoners and the tortured.' But I consoled myself with the idea that, in being the Archbishop of the prisoners and the tortured, I was being the Archbishop of the city."[24]

To promote social justice, the cardinal launched initiatives on several fronts in 1973. His first act was to sell the luxurious residence in which he had been living and to move to a more modest address. The proceeds of this sale were used to build community centers on the periphery of São Paulo and thus to stimulate the formation of CEBs and other popular self-help organizations.[25] During 1973, as well, Dom Paulo distributed 150,000 copies of the "Universal Declaration of Human Rights," a United Nations document to which Brazil had been a signatory. By 1979, then in its fourth printing, the number of pamphlets circulated throughout the archdiocese had reached one million.[26]

Beginning in the mid 1970s, Cardinal Arns also oversaw the creation of various archdiocesan councils and commissions with specialized human-rights-related mandates. Among the most important of those established were the Archdiocesan Commission of the Pastoral of Human Rights and the Marginalized, and the Justice and Peace Commission. The former body has fulfilled an important pedagogical function and, among its many accomplishments, has prepared and distributed an extremely detailed account of repressive actions taken against Church workers, entitled *Repressão a Igreja do Brasil: Reflexão sobre uma situação de opressão, 1968–78* (Repression of the Church in Brazil: Reflection on a situation of oppression, 1968–78).[27] The Justice and Peace Commission has been intensely involved in the publication of human-rights material for popular consumption, in pointing out specific violations of basic freedoms, and in providing legal assistance for those who required it.[28] In addition, as early as 1975, it released a scathing report on the reality of economic and racial inequality in the archdiocese in a book entitled *São Paulo: Crescimento e probreza* (São Paulo: Growth and poverty).

Another important initiative was the creation of the archdiocesan Workers' Pastoral, which, together with several members of the hierarchy, was instrumental in aiding thousands of striking metalworkers in São Paulo's industrial belt during 1980. The metalworkers had walked off their jobs to press for higher wages, but their strike was declared illegal by state authorities. This resulted in a standoff between the strikers and local military officials, who eventually resorted to the use of force in anticipation of disorderly protest.[29] Working at the grass-roots level, the Workers' Pastoral maintained a coordinating function. Specifically, it helped to arrange meetings between union leaders and ensured that each of the regional bargaining fronts involved in the strike was accompanied by a representative of the Church.[30] These actions were backed up by various pronouncements and homilies, and by the publication of open letters signed by Dom Paulo and other bishops.[31] Members of the hierarchy also provided strategic and material help in the form of parish halls and churches, which were freely made available for the strikers.

Two years later, during the general elections of 1982, the Workers' Pastoral and other Church agencies mobilized to educate the electorate about voting procedures and party platforms. To this end, a number of instructional pamphlets were prepared and distributed throughout the São Paulo area. The most important of these was a booklet entitled *Fé e política* (Faith and politics), produced by the Human Rights Pastoral. Without favoring any party, this publication provided a clear and concise political history of Brazil, emphasizing the importance of the people's involvement in the democratic process.

Finally, the Human Rights and other pastorals were very active during the popular campaign for the direct presidential vote in 1984. The immediate objective of this nationwide campaign, which was orchestrated by the country's opposition parties between January and May 1984, was to force the Congress to pass a bill abolishing the existing electoral college.[32] In São Paulo, lay and clerical activists circulated petitions, promoted attendance at rallies, held debates, and generally kept election talk alive in the churches and the CEBs.[33]

Aside from the various pastoral task forces Dom Paulo created, the proclamations he issued, and the multitude of individual actions he initiated or promoted during his first 15 years as archbishop of São Paulo, two other developments sponsored by the cardinal stand out as having had extremely positive implications for the implementation of the "option for the poor." Both were related to the operation of the archdiocese.

The first significant development occurred after Cardinal Arns divided the archdiocese into nine separate episcopal regions. Fully functional by the late 1970s, these regions were designated as quasidioceses, with their own curiae, office personnel, and resident bishops.

One immediate result of this division was the improvement of decision-making and command structures in the archdiocese. On the one hand, lay and clerical input from the parishes was now channeled through the various regional offices, and thus lent a degree of additional weight. On the other hand, directives from the central curia were now implemented by an intermediary bureaucracy, which had the power to modify or increase their impact in accordance with local needs or desires.

The creation of separate regions, and the appointment of auxiliary bishops to run them, also contributed to the moral "presence" of the Church in São Paulo. Instead of just one archbishop proclaiming the cause of the poor and oppressed, nine voices were added to the chorus, each representing a clearly definable constituency. Over the years, two bishops in particular have become almost legendary crusaders in aid of the lower classes. The first of these is Dom Luciano Mendes de Almeida, the former bishop of Belém region, who went on to become president of the CNBB. The second outspoken bishop is Dom Angélico Sândalo Bernardino, formerly of São Miguel region. A virulent critic of the military, Dom Angélico edited several progressive publications in the archdiocese and personally led numerous protest marches through the streets of eastern São Paulo in open defiance of the authorities.

Finally, the territorial division of the archdiocese undertaken by Cardinal Arns greatly stimulated the pastoral work of the Church in São Paulo. Each region, for example, maintained its own set of pastoral programs, which were defined and oriented with an eye to resolving local problems. Representatives from the various regional teams, moreover, were active within the pastoral task forces and commissions that operated at the archdiocesan level, thus contributing to the articulation and execution of more broadly based goals and activities.

In connection with their pastoral programs, most of the regions also published a variety of materials for popular use. Some of these were destined for local use only, some exported to other specific regions, and some distributed throughout the archdiocese. The region of São Miguel, for instance, maintained its own publishing facility, the Centro de Comunicações e Educação Popular (Center for Communications and Popular Education). This organization produced the region's monthly newspaper, *Grita povo* (Cry of the people), and other books and pamphlets for use in the CEBs and churches. It also published material for various popular movements with only informal Church ties. Through the Center, for example, the Movement against Unemployment in São Miguel prepared and distributed its newsletter, *De olho no desemprego* (Eye on unemployment). In another region, Osasco, a team of volunteer priests, nuns, and laypersons, produced everything from a monthly *Boletim informativo* (Informative bulletin) to a 32-part correspondence course in theology. The team is especially proud of the voluminous material preaching the Church's "preferential option for the poor," which it published for use in regional catechism classes.

The other major change in the organizational structure of the archdiocese was the establishment of joint pastoral planning after 1975. Since that time, drawing on input from a broad spectrum of religious and lay sectors within the Church, a number of programs and initiatives have been put into place. All in all, 18 areas for pastoral attention have been defined over the years, from the Workers and Human Rights pastorals to agencies dealing with health care and abandoned children. All such pastorals independently coordinate activities, arrange conferences, and disseminate information on topics their respective spheres of action.

Through joint pastoral planning, the archdiocese has also been able to define areas for priority action in São Paulo. The identification of these areas has served to target and intensify the work of the Church where it is most needed and, in a more general sense, "to awaken Christians and others so that they might articulate, promote, and defend human rights as a response to the requirements of the Gospel."[34]

Between 1975 and 1980, the four programs that were consistently singled out for attention were the following: (1) the Pastoral of Human Rights and the Marginalized, (2) the Workers' Pastoral, (3) the Pastoral of the Periphery, and (4) the comunidades eclesiais de base—the CEBs.

CEB promotion in the Archdiocese of São Paulo

To say that the CEBs have consistently been a priority in São Paulo is probably, in fact, something of an understatement, given the long-standing and stalwart commitment the Church has made to the CEB phenomenon. Since at least 1973, when Cardinal Arns sold the episcopal palace to liberate funds for the construction of CEB community centers on the periphery, the Church has invested a considerable portion of its manpower and resources in the promotion and activation of the groups.

In official Church documents, the overwhelming attention given the CEBs has been justified in a number of ways. First, in the face of a rather inappropriate urban parish system, the CEBs are seen as enhancing the presence of the Church in the community. Second, they are interpreted as stimulating a distinct form of the human fellowship for which the universal Church stands. Third, the groups are seen as a concrete expression of the Church's "preferential option for the poor." And finally, they are envisioned as offering opportunities for the realization of both traditional and innovative Church goals such as evangelization, sharing, personal growth, and, ultimately, the transformation of both ecclesial and sociopolitical structures.[35]

Recent statements made by Cardinal Arns also help to explain the importance accorded CEB formation and growth in São Paulo.[36] According to Dom Paulo, the CEBs must be seen as a phenomenon predominantly of the people and for the people. Moreover, as a direct consequence of their essential character, states the cardinal, they possess a unique religious and social thrust. In the religious sphere, the CEBs have restored the historic role of the laypeople in the governance of the Church and are helping to renew and rebuild outmoded institutional structures such as the parish. "The path of the CEBs has brought forth," asserts Cardinal Arns, "without a shadow of a doubt, a breeze of evangelical renovation within the Church as an institution. It gives back to the people their role within the Church, reformulates the services and ministries, and encourages co-operation in the coordination of pastoral decisions." In the secular sphere, he adds, the groups help awaken the poor to the necessity of organized action, and make an invaluable contribution to the amelioration of social conditions. In essence, he states, they "have made possible increased critical consciousness in the face of reality, and have motivated new forms of organization, greatly contributing to the betterment of living conditions, especially for the population of the periphery, which through them have felt motivated to fight for their rights."

For Cardinal Arns, participation in the CEBs thus has a liberating function—neither exclusively religious nor exclusively political, but encompassing both realms. In his words, this liberating role is "the heart of the CEBs, seeing that in [them, the people] identify themselves with the purpose of Christ who came to evangelize among the poor, and who affirmed that the Kingdom of Heaven was theirs. [Here], there is no opposition between faith and politics, because there was also no division in the practice or teaching of Jesus."

Dimensions of the CEB presence

Whatever the reasons behind the official support of the CEBs in São Paulo, there is little doubt that such encouragement has contributed to a thriving and active CEB presence in the archdiocese, and over a very short period of time. Since the groups appeared in the 1960s, they have multiplied at an incredible pace. In 1980, when the first official count was undertaken, there were approximately 470 CEBs registered in all parts of the city. By 1983, this number had grown to 765, and by late 1988, to 938.[37] This represents an annual growth rate of at least 10 percent.

Table 1 summarizes data on CEB strength during the years 1980, 1983, and 1988 for each of the nine episcopal regions of the archdiocese. Using 1983 divisions to facilitate comparison, these are broken down further into a total of 48 sectors.[38] Information is also presented on the socioeconomic status of the sector (1=most affluent, 8=poorest) and the mean age of pastors working in the field in 1983.[39]

It becomes immediately apparent that the CEBs have been growing in recent years in all areas of São Paulo (with the exception of Sé region). Nevertheless, some regions, quite obviously, have more CEBs than others—considerably more, in some cases—in all years.

In some respects, the pattern that is revealed is explained by the very nature of the "option for the poor" itself. As, in fact, one might ex-

Table 1. Number of CEBs in the Episcopal Regions of
the Archdiocese of São Paulo, 1980, 1983, 1988

Region and sector	Socio-economic score	Mean age of pastors	1980	1983	1988
Região Sé					
Aclimação	2	66	—	—	—
Catedral	4	60	—	—	—
Cerqueira Cesar	2	55	—	—	—
Parí	4	60	—	—	—
Pinheiros	1	60	—	—	—
Santa Cecília	1	56	12	12	—
Santo Amaro					
Cupecê*	7	48	13	10	25
Interlagos*	8	46	40	32	74
Sabará*	7	49	6	7	31
Santo Amaro	5	53	3	3	9
Itapecerica da Serra					
Campo Limpo*	7	54	21	45	25
Capão Redondo*	8	55	37	58	68
Itapecerica da Serra*	8	40	36	52	48
Morumbi	5	50	7	9	10
São Miguel					
Artur Alvim	6	39	7	10	15
Cangaíba	6	39	1	5	8
Guaianazes	8	53	10	16	28
Itaim Paulista	8	49	18	21	26
Itaquera*	8	39	9	32	35
Ponte Rasa	8	39	10	13	11
São Miguel	8	45	14	23	24
Vila Esperança	6	50	2	—	1
Santana					
Casa Verde	6	53	4	9	—
Mandaqui	5	57	6	7	13
Santana	5	58	4	13	12
Tremenbé	6	56	11	13	8
Tucuruvi	6	55	4	4	4
Vila Maria	6	53	8	10	11
Belém					
Belém	4	54	n.a.	—	4
São Mateus	8	37	n.a.	27	40

Table 1—*Continued*

Region and sector	Socio-economic score	Mean age of pastors	1980	1983	1988
Sapopemba	8	56	n.a.	28	42
Tatuapé	5	55	n.a.	—	1
Vila Formosa	6	53	n.a.	—	9
Vila Prudente	7	52	n.a.	16	15
Lapa					
Brasilândia	8	45	16	19	27
Butantã	5	44	10	16	17
Freguesia do Ó	7	52	2	7	9
Lapa	4	57	6	3	7
Pereira Barreto	8	52	17	26	32
Pirituba	7	47	5	11	5
Osasco					
Barueri*	8	52	36	51	61
Bonfim	7	52	18	25	34
Santo Antonio	7	51	20	27	34
São Roque*	8	44	42	88	94
Ipiranga					
Anchieta	5	54	4	3	4
Imigrantes	7	46	11	14	17
Ipiranga	3	57	—	—	—
Vila Mariana	3	57	—	—	—

*Sectors that were divided after 1983

pect, the CEBs tend to proliferate among those people toward whom the "option" is directed—that is, the lower classes. Although the groups are certainly not absent in more affluent sectors (socioeconomic status 1 to 5), such as Mandaqui and Morumbi, they are much more likely to be abundant in areas with much lower scores, such as Capão Redondo and São Roque. Confirming this observation, positive and highly significant Pearson correlation scores of between .60 and .70 were found to exist between socioeconomic status and CEB strength for all years.

To some extent, the variation exhibited in the table is also attributable to one of the ways in which CEB activation has been encouraged in São Paulo—that is, through the participation of younger, more politically progressive priests who serve as pastoral agents for the Church. In 1983, a significant correlation of $-.38$ was found to exist between the mean age of pastors in any given sector and the number of CEBs present, indicating that the CEBs proliferate not only among the poor, but potentially anywhere where Church personnel are posted who are ostensibly more in tune with the "option for the poor."

Conclusion

São Paulo is not all of Brazil, nor is Brazil only São Paulo. Yet, in many ways the area is a microcosm of Brazilian society and is truly reflective of its many contrasts. It is both highly industrialized and rural, rich and poor, sophisticated and humble; both a success, in terms of development, and a failure.

Within the overarching structure of the Brazilian Catholic Church, São Paulo is also extremely important. Before its breakup in 1989, the archdiocese of São Paulo was by far the largest in Brazil. And in executing the Church's commitment to the "preferential option for the poor," São Paulo took the lead in implementing a number of key strategies—most important, the CEBs, which have enjoyed tremendous stimulation and growth in the fertile territory of the archdiocese.

3
Functions and Activities

—

Because of São Paulo's commitment to the CEBs and the large number of groups known to exist there, the archdiocese provides an excellent venue for CEB-related research. It offers an appropriate and an important frame of reference for examining both the essential nature of the groups and their sociopolitical impact.

Consequently, in 1984, 22 CEBs were selected from within this ecclesiastical unit to be the subject of an in-depth investigation of the CEB phenomenon in all of its integral aspects. During the first six months of that year, these groups were subjected to intense examination, with particular attention paid to their activities, organization, and politico-religious orientation. Precisely four years later, in the spring of 1988, the same set of CEBs—of which 20 were still in existence—were reexamined and the progress of individual groups was assessed.

In both 1984 and 1988, the attitudes and behavior of ordinary CEB members were also examined, using a self-administered questionnaire. In 1984, respondents were drawn from all 22 groups and numbered 275. In 1988, a much smaller group of 69 were investigated. These were members of a subset of more politically active CEBs, which will be examined in detail beginning in chapter 7.[1]

Following a stratified random-sampling plan, the CEBs in question were chosen from a variety of settings representing basic social-class and geopolitical divisions of the São Paulo area. Eleven of the sample groups were selected from lower-class residential areas. Of these, 9 were situated on the working-class periphery of the city, and 2 were in slum areas near São Paulo's urban core. The remaining 11 CEBs in the sample were resident in more affluent, middle-class areas in various parts of the city.

In 1984, the ages of the sample CEBs ranged from less than 1 year to 17 years, for an average of approximately 6 years. Membership ranged from 5 to 50, with an average of 22. By 1988, average age within the sample had increased to 11, whereas average membership had decreased to about 18.

Basic activities

Given the rather limited sampling frame, that is, the archdiocese of São Paulo, these CEBs obviously cannot be said to represent all groups in Brazil—especially those operating far from urban areas. Nevertheless, they were chosen from a wide variety of conditions and circumstances and thus provide a rich source of data.

This variety is perhaps no more evident than with respect to basic group function. Here, the sample reveals the CEBs to be engaged in a broad range of undertakings, as indeed some of the CEB literature has already affirmed. Authors such as Heléna Salem and Mainwaring, for example, have pointed to a very diverse pattern of both religious and political involvement within Brazilian CEBs generally.[2]

In the realm of strictly traditional, or devotional, activities, to begin with, the São Paulo CEBs demonstrate considerable diversity. One of the more common functions is charity work, which usually involves the collection and distribution of money, food, clothing, or medicine to those in the surrounding area who might not otherwise be able to afford it. Charity work might also involve funding or helping to run child-care facilities in poor neighborhoods, or visiting the sick or disabled. Bible study, intended to stimulate greater knowledge of the Scriptures, is another popular CEB activity. Sometimes this is undertaken in conjunction with holy days, such as Easter and Christmas, but might simply involve the random selection of passages for reading and interpretation. The CEBs also offer catechism classes to instruct the young in the basic principles of the Catholic faith. Sometimes these are conducted by group members themselves, and sometimes by nuns or seminarians as available. Finally, the CEBs often plan and hold festivals, or bazaars. Such events are usually (but not necessarily) held on or near periods of religious or national significance. Sometimes they are planned simply for the diversion and entertainment of local residents. Other times, they are a useful fund-raising vehicle.

Together with these standard types of devotional activities, the CEBs frequently engage in a fair number of more innovative functions. These have largely emerged in the progressive wake of Vatican II, and many have become synonymous with the Brazilian CEB phenomenon.

Without question, the most popular of these is the preparation and offering of local *celebrações*. These services are akin to the Mass, but are usually less formal and tend to be led by lay ministers or nuns as opposed to priests. Many times, as well, they are conducted using liturgical pamphlets prepared by the local Church or specific religious congregations. In São Paulo, two very popular pamphlets of this type are *O Domingo* (Sunday) and *Todos irmãos* (All brothers). Preparation for and of certain other sacraments is also undertaken in many groups. A baptism, for instance, might involve the establishment of preparatory courses for parents, and planning with regard to when and how the act itself will be undertaken during a religious service. Reflection and discussion constitute another popular CEB standard. Though somewhat similar to Bible study, this activity usually offers participants a much greater opportunity to discuss the relevance of Biblical passages to everyday life. Quite often, as in the case of the celebrações, specially prepared pamphlets and other didactic materials are used to facilitate the process. A related CEB function, *conscientização* (which I have translated as consciousness raising), consists of somewhat more in-depth discussion and debate regarding the reality of social, economic, and political oppression—locally, nationally, or even internationally. This may be conducted with direct reference to Scripture or, here again, to specially prepared pedagogical material.

Three additional activities of the innovative type are more pragmatic in nature. The first is the development of craft skills such as knitting and crochet and carpentry. Members may participate for pure enjoyment or fraternity, but they can often use knowledge obtained to save money or earn income for their families. A second pragmatic activity is literacy training, which utilizes the now-famous Paulo Freire method.[3] In theory at least, this involves a dialectical exchange between teacher and learner as equals, and draws heavily on the everyday experience of oppression for its instructional material.

The third and final type of pragmatic activity consists of the *revindicações*, or community-action projects. These are perhaps the most politically explicit functions that the CEBs undertake with any regularity. Among the lower classes, the community projects are normally designed to secure basic services, infrastructural improvements, or legal land title for residents in the local area. In more affluent urban neighborhoods, community action usually takes a less dramatic form, perhaps involving *mutirões* (joint-labor initiatives), neighborhood crime watches, food cooperatives, or even CEB promotion itself.

In all cases, however, the method used in the execution of these projects is the same and involves a considerable amount of group coordination. To begin with, group members must be called together to discuss some problem at hand. If it is determined to be of serious enough consequence, the problem is then written up and attached to a petition, which is circulated throughout the immediate area. When sufficient signatures are obtained, a delegation of CEB members is selected to meet with the appropriate government authorities. At these meetings, a statement of intent regarding the means for resolving the CEB's complaint is usually obtained from the official, as well as a deadline for remedial work to begin. This accomplished, CEB members then wait for the official involved to take action, or for the negotiated start-up date to pass. When the latter occurs, as it frequently does, CEB members are dispatched in increasing numbers to subsequently planned encounters, thus putting continual pressure on the government agent to resolve their complaint.

It should be pointed out that aside from the revindicações, the CEBs, both within and outside the São Paulo sample, do, occasionally at least, engage in other forms of explicit political behavior. CEBs and CEB members do, for example, become involved in urban protest movements calling for the establishing or improvement of services such as health care, busing, or policing. Sometimes these movements are directed from within the Church itself (usually at the diocesan level), and sometimes they are secular in nature.[4] The CEBs have also been known to assist striking workers. During the São Paulo metalworkers' strikes of 1979–1980, many CEBs offered both moral and material support to the strikers and their families. In addition, some CEBs, in both rural and urban areas, have even engaged in land invasions, taking over unused public and private property to either farm or construct housing. Finally, some CEBs have become directly involved in political campaigns on behalf of specific parties—although such action has rarely been sanctioned by the Church. As Ricardo Galletta points out, many CEB members from all parts of Brazil ran as candidates in the 1982 Brazilian general elections, mostly for the left-of-center Partido dos Trabalhadores (Workers' Party).[5]

Nevertheless, although it is important, such activity tends to be somewhat transitory. Though exceptions do exist—such as in the case of those rural CEBs most heavily involved in land disputes—available evidence suggests that such actions do not become core preoccupations for individual CEBs over the long term. More than any other single activity,

Table 2. Activity Profile of CEBs, 1984 and 1988
(Percentages in Parentheses)

Activity	Number of groups participating, 1984 (n=22)		Number of groups participating, 1988 (n=20)	
Traditional activities:				
Charity work	11	(50)	14	(70)
Bible study	11	(50)	18	(90)
Religious festive days	11	(50)	13	(65)
Innovative activities:				
Local celebrações	12	(55)	12	(60)
Preparation of celebrações	10	(45)	11	(55)
Preparation for other sacraments	7	(32)	11	(55)
Reflection and discussion	19	(86)	18	(90)
Consciousness raising	8	(36)	9	(45)
Community action	10	(45)	11	(55)

the community-action projects, or revindicações, still represent the best opportunity for regular political involvement for the largest number of group members.

Activity preferences

Not all of the activities undertaken by the CEBs, of course, are carried out by all groups at all times. Rather, the CEBs are quite selective about the functions they will or will not routinely undertake. This, in fact, is what gives the phenomenon a very heterogeneous character, which is all too frequently overlooked.

For the São Paulo sample, the degree of heterogeneity of activity preferences is revealed in Table 2. In the table, data are presented on the frequency with which specific activities were undertaken on a regular basis in both 1984 and 1988.

Initial observations from 1984 clearly show some activities to have been more popular than others among the 22 groups sampled. The celebrações and their preparation, as well as all of the more traditional activities, appealed to only one-half of the groups. Moreover, whereas nearly all the CEBs in 1984 were engaged in reflection and discussion, only about one-half involved themselves in the community-action projects. Sacrament preparation and consciousness raising were also among the less popular activities, with about one-third of the groups engaged.

By 1988, these differences had diminished to some extent. In fact, a rise in popularity appears to have occurred for almost every activity category, involving either the regularization of activities formerly undertaken on a casual basis, or the adoption of completely new ones. Such a change in popularity is especially noteworthy in the case of the more traditional functions, but is also apparent for explicitly political activities such as consciousness raising and the revindicações.

What this seems to point to is the emergence of a more rounded, or mature, CEB phenomenon in which groups engage in a broader range of activities. This is not to suggest, however, that the groups are necessarily becoming more homogenous. What must still be considered is the way in which functions are combined in individual groups, as well as the popularity of certain types of activities among CEB members.

Activity combinations and group types

Where combinations of group activities are concerned, first of all, a good deal of mixing does occur within the CEBs. This ensures that no two CEBs will be the same.

Even so, a limited number of general CEB types can be constructed. These are, in essence, "ideal-types," in the Weberian sense of the term, and though they cannot possibly capture the full range of group diversity, they are useful for reference and comparison.

The most elementary kinds of CEBs that can be discerned from the sample can be described as *simple devotional groups* (Type I). In such CEBs, only more elementary forms of religious activity—such as Bible study, charity work, and sometimes biblical reflection—are practiced by members. Political activities, such as consciousness raising and community-action projects, are generally avoided.

Devotional miniparishes (Type II) are a slightly more evolved type of CEB. Such groups generally avoid political activity, but along with more elementary devotional practices, often engage in a variety of more innovative religious functions. Aside from Bible study and charity work, for example, CEBs of this type hold weekly celebrações for local residents, offer baptisms and baptismal-preparation classes, and, of course, actively engage in biblical reflection.

A third CEB type, the *elementary devotional and political CEB* (Type

III), has much in common with the *simple devotional group* with respect to the rather limited type and breadth of religious activities offered. What distinguishes this CEB category, however, is its limited involvement in certain political activities —namely, consciousness raising.

Politically oriented miniparishes (Type IV) are more advanced in terms of both religious and political activities than the types examined thus far. They tend, first of all, to engage in the full slate of traditional and innovative religious activities undertaken by the *devotional miniparishes*. In addition, CEBs of this type participate in a fairly extensive range of political functions. These include not only consciousness raising, but, to a limited extent, certain elementary community-action projects. For instance, they might be involved in the establishment of food cooperatives, crime watches, or joint-labor initiatives.

A fifth and much more explicitly politically active group type is the *politically oriented missionary CEB* (Type V). These groups tend, in fact, to be almost totally unconcerned with most religious practices. Celebrações and even biblical reflection are held only infrequently. Most of the group's energy is directed toward the community-action projects or toward CEB promotion, which is often undertaken in less affluent neighborhoods located at some distance from the group itself.

The last CEB type, the *classical, or ideal-typical, CEB* (Type VI) is the one that comes closest to the description of the groups that appears again and again in the liberationist literature. CEBs of this category strongly resemble the *politically oriented miniparish* in all but one respect: the quality of the political activity undertaken. Whereas *politically oriented miniparish* CEBs engage in rather more basic forms of community action, the *classical* CEBs are all deeply involved in the neighborhood-improvement projects described earlier. Such activities are not, however, it should be cautioned, carried out at the expense of more religious practices such as the celebrações, baptismal preparation, or even charity work. For the most part, both traditional and innovative religious activities remain at the core of the groups' activity offerings.

Member-participation rates

The São Paulo sample also exemplifies the diversifying effect of the activity preferences of CEB members themselves. Indeed, it would appear that just as certain functions are more likely to be undertaken in some groups or group types, so too are members themselves differentially disposed to engage in various practices, thus restricting inter-CEB homogeneity.

Table 3. CEB-Member Participation Rates for Selected Activities,
1984 (in Percentages) (n=275)

Activity	Regularly	Sometimes	Not at all*
Traditional activities:			
Charity	42	31	27
Bible study	51	31	18
Innovative activities:			
Preparation of celebrações	36	21	43
Reflection	55	20	25
Consciousness raising	23	28	49

*Includes "don't know," "not applicable," and missing responses.

In 1984, for example, as can be seen from Table 3, regular participation in biblical reflection was considerably higher than that for charity work. Conversely, preparation for the celebrações and involvement in consciousness raising were avoided by far more members than was Bible study.

Even when examination of participation rates is restricted to only those groups that offered the activities in question, a similar pattern is revealed. Whereas about 70 percent of the membership in groups offering reflection and discussion participated regularly or sometimes in this activity, only about half of these groups' members participated in charity work where this was offered. Similarly, where the regular and occasional participation rate for Bible study in groups offering the activity was about 60 percent, this fell to less than 40 percent for consciousness raising.

From 1984 to 1988, little seems to have changed in this regard. Even though the proportions of group members involved in specific activities were generally higher in the 1988 membership sample, the differences in activity preference remained. For example, in groups offering the preparation of celebrações, reflection, and/or sacrament preparation, participation for the former two functions was over 70 percent, but only 45 percent for the latter. Charity work, similarly, attracted nearly three-quarters of available participants, and consciousness raising drew slightly over half.

In many cases, it might be noted as well, variations in member participation are also symptomatic of considerable *intragroup* heterogeneity— even conflict. Usually, disputes center around members' assessments of the appropriateness of certain activities, especially those of a political character. More traditional Catholics, for whom the CEBs simply represent a new way of worshiping, often feel threatened and angered by more innovative forms of political involvement undertaken by progressives. As a direct consequence, they often avoid activities deemed too radical. By the same token, many progressive CEB members find more devotional activities to be somewhat irrelevant. In part, at least, such division is readily revealed in members' assessments of which activities should receive priority and which should be dropped. When asked specifically about whether they would like a change in emphasis within their own group from more devotional to more innovative activities, for example, respondents from the São Paulo CEBs were almost evenly divided in their opinion.

Another example of the dynamics of such conflict can be found in one of the sample CEBs in particular, the Comunidade Santa Maria. Some members of this group were very much dismayed by the involvement of two group leaders in the local chapter of the left-wing Partido dos Trabalhadores. One of the leaders, in fact, had even run as a candidate for the PT in the 1982 elections, in direct contravention of Church directives. As a result of their displeasure, more traditional group members simply avoided participation in activities even remotely political, even the weekly celebrações. A more conservative CEB leader explained, "There is a problem with political parties within the group. The fight began when they introduced politics into the mass. This weakened everything. Many people just stayed away."

In other groups, more traditional group members react in subtler ways to controversial activities offered by their CEBs. Instead of completely withdrawing from certain functions, they simply fail to participate fully when called upon. For example, many CEB members may claim to engage in consciousness raising, but in fact refuse to utter a single word during encounters. Indeed, the encouragement of member participation, especially where less politically oriented Catholics are concerned, is a major problem in many groups. It is more often than not a considerable challenge for pastoral agents and group leaders to get people to discuss social and political problems openly. Quite often, whether in the *consciousness-raising* sessions or following the homily at the *celebrações*, participation is restricted to a very few players who are already somewhat politically aware.

Aside from their negative effect on intra-CEB heterogeneity, members' disputes over participation in certain activities also affect the CEBs' this-worldly political involvement, as one might imagine. This particular aspect of member disagreement, however, will be discussed in detail in chapter 7.

Conclusion

The CEBs are a very complex and heterogeneous collectivity in terms of the activities they undertake. Significantly, as well, differences between groups or group types with respect to function are often matched by variation within groups—variation traced, for the most part, to widely divergent activity preferences among the membership.

Where there exist such divergencies, especially of the latter type, tensions can naturally arise—and, in fact, these are not uncommon in the CEBs. Ultimately, such disputes and tensions are resolved within the realms of organization, leadership, and control. Yet, even these areas themselves are sources of frequent controversy, as will be shown.

4
Organization, Leadership, and Control
-

Because of their functional complexity and broad range of member interests, the CEBs—like most other types of organization—require some form of internal structure and control. The precise forms that CEB organization and leadership take, however, are at least as varied as the functions they are designed to support. The only constant, perhaps, is the way in which the CEBs relate to the larger institution of the Roman Catholic Church.

Internal organization
A range of options are evident in the organizational strategies operating within the CEBs. These are clearly demonstrated in the São Paulo sample, where, in effect, each group has devised a somewhat unique strategy for bringing members together to undertake specific activities in specific ways, at specific places and times.

Regarding, first of all, the coordination of specific CEB activities, two basic patterns emerge. Some groups, particularly those of smaller size, tend to involve all members directly in specific functions undertaken at various times throughout the month or year. Larger CEBs, by contrast, tend to maintain auxiliary subgroups, or teams, that are given responsibility for coordinating group activities or for undertaking these in a more intimate setting. Both in 1984 and 1988, about half of the São Paulo CEBs fell into this second category, each possessing a number of subgroups to coordinate things like sacrament preparation and catechism classes, or simply to engage in biblical reflection or consciousness raising.

In carrying out their various functions, a few groups also utilize what is a more recent organizational innovation—the *grupos de rua*. These are small, informal discussion groups organized by the CEB during special times of year such as Easter and Christmas. Present in about one-third of the sample CEBs in both 1984 and 1988, they are designed to take the CEB even closer to the people, so to speak, and to stimulate the growth of new groups throughout the local area. In some cases, as well, although this was not evident in the sample itself, the grupo de rua strategy has been taken even further. In parts of São Miguel Episcopal Region, for example, the entire parish was designated as the comunidade, with much smaller lay cells—which would otherwise be known as CEBs—taking the grupo de rua label.

As for CEB meeting places, considerable diversity is in evidence. Some of the CEBs in the sample met in members' homes, whereas others used local church facilities. By 1988, about half of the CEBs, as well, owned their own community center. Constructed with group funds on Church-owned land, these buildings are a focal point for the CEBs, providing one central location for all group activities.

The frequency of these meetings also varies greatly, from once a month, to once a week, even to once every several days, depending on the variety and the number of teams in operation within the CEB. In many groups, at least some of these encounters are full-membership meetings, called to discuss the progress of group activities and/or plans for future engagement. The frequency of such gatherings, however, appears to be diminishing over the years as the groups become more diversified. In 1984, about half of the CEBs held weekly membership meetings, but by 1988, this number had fallen to less than one-third.

Leadership and direction

Within the organizational structure of the CEB, the actual coordination of group functions by leaders or directors operates differently at different levels. Specific activities, first of all, such as charity work or Bible study, are typically coordinated by interested volunteers. And sometimes—this is especially true for more devotional activities—leadership functions are undertaken by lay ministers, trained at the diocesan level. In the São Paulo sample, lay ministers were active in about two-thirds of the groups, taking charge of such things as sacrament preparation, reflection groups, and, most important, the celebrações.

Patterns of administration at the group level are somewhat more complex. In the literature, it is true, the CEBs are frequently upheld as paragons of direct democracy, involving all members in the process of debate and decision making regarding everything from mass preparation to revenue collection to paying the bills incurred by the local community center. In reality, however, this is rarely the case. The fact is that individual CEBs can be as oligarchic or democratic as any other similar type of religious or secular association.

In the São Paulo sample, about half the CEBs conform to the democratic ideal, insofar as they have representative councils, or *conselhos*, as they are called. Participation in these governing bodies can be quite high, involving more than two-thirds of group members. Usually, however, the conselho counts from about 8 to about 15 participants. Sometimes these are elected by direct ballot, and sometimes they are self-appointed, depending on the group. Granted, the mere existence of such councils does not guarantee a measure of democratic decision making. Nevertheless, it does certainly suggest a strong commitment to more cooperative forms of governance.

Some CEBs that have no such governing councils are more autocratically run. In some cases, the membership simply appoints one of its own as leader. Authority is then delegated to this individual, who, in turn, is expected to act in the best interests of the membership. Another option is direct governance by the local Church. In this case, the membership simply looks to the local priest or nun for direction or, failing that, will accept a clerically appointed layperson.

This latter set of options, it should be pointed out, does not necessarily preclude an element of direct democracy. Even when representative government is missing, lay members are still able to exercise a certain amount of control in matters affecting the direction and organization of their group. In fact, they are often strongly encouraged to do so. Nevertheless, the reins of power tend to remain in the hands of a minority who have the freedom to impose their wishes on the membership at large.

Dimensions of ecclesiastical control

Regardless of the type of formal leadership extant within the CEBs, at root it is the institutional Church that provides the most enduring and pervasive source of guidance for the groups. To be sure, the CEBs are creatures of the Church and, to a considerable extent, are subject to its dictates.

In São Paulo, the Church has gone to great lengths to emphasize the necessity and importance of firm CEB-institutional links. Even Cardinal Arns, a strong supporter of autonomous CEB action in the secular sphere, has emphasized the necessity of maintaining a close bond between the CEBs and the mother Church. Though the cardinal admits that the CEBs are "born of the wish of the oppressed . . . for liberation," he carefully adds that this "experience drinks from the fountain of a new conception of the Church as dictated by Vatican II."[1] Thus, the CEBs do not exist outside of the Church, but neither are they simply subordinated to it. Instead, Dom Paulo insists, the CEBs "are the Church"[2] and as such must stand "always united with their priests and bishops."[3]

During interviews with the auxiliary bishops who presided over the nine episcopal regions that constituted the archdiocese up to 1989, this preoccupation with the maintenance of strong ecclesiastical ties was replicated for the most part. The bishops expressed concerns identical to those of Cardinal Arns, arguing that the groups should be thought of as a strictly ecclesial phenomenon, born within the Church and subject to the authority of the hierarchy. As they clearly stated in a 1982 joint publication, "The CEB is not an exogenous nucleus that seeks to incorporate itself into the ecclesial body. It is not a competitive vanguard, in conflict with the hierarchical structure. It is not a political group in search of easy cover or desirous of using the Church. The CEB in Brazil is the Church."[4]

Where disagreement among the bishops was apparent, it was usually about the degree to which Church-CEB solidarity must be actively maintained by the institution. Some of the bishops were less convinced that active intervention on this front was necessary, maintaining that the people themselves adamantly insist on a hierarchical presence within the groups. Others tended to emphasize the importance of forging Church-CEB links in a direct and forceful manner. The general feeling among this group is perhaps best expressed in a comment made by Dom Alfredo Novak of Lapa region: "The ecclesial component [of the groups] is very important. What we are defending here is a tripartite notion of the CEBs. . . . The CEB is a communion between the priest, the people and the bishop."[5]

The principal fear among those bishops adhering to such a view was that without constant hierarchical vigilance, the CEBs might fall prey to manipulation by secular forces and thus move away from the Church. In their minds, the threat of CEB instrumentalization from both the right and the left of the political spectrum was a clear and present danger, as the following comments demonstrate.

> It [manipulation] is an element which must be taken up by the fathers of the spirit; people have to discuss the possibility.[6]

> We know the people who like to do this [instrumentalize the CEBs]. Sometimes we have to speak to them, and to the groups, but it is difficult.[7]

The groups are subject to manipulation from the right and the left. The people often can't tell the difference. . . . Attacks on supermarkets, bus burnings, and so forth are all the result of manipulation.[8]

Those organizations most interested in using the CEBs for their own purposes, claimed the bishop of Santana, Dom Joel Capatan, are the ideologues of the military regime, the Workers' Party, and revolutionary groups such as the Brazilian Community Party (PCB) and the Marxist guerilla cell known as MR-8.[9]

A similar sentiment regarding ecclesiastical control was found among 22 Church personnel and pastoral agents interviewed in São Paulo during the course of the research on the CEBs. Like the bishops, the majority of these individuals agreed that the CEBs are not properly constituted in the absence of Church representatives. Only 2 of the 10 periphery-based clerics and nuns were of the view that the presence of a pastoral agent is not always necessary.

In addition, about half of these interviewees expressed views similar to those of some bishops that active clerical supervision is required to ward off the threat of CEB manipulation emanating from secular sources. Left-wing political groups were most frequently mentioned as the perpetrators of CEB subversion. The CEBs, stated one priest, were in fact "easily manipulated by the left, people without faith." "They speak badly of the Church," he added, "but they use it." A nun who had been working with *favelados* (slum-dwellers) was more specific about the perpetrators of manipulation, pointing the finger at one group in particular. "One time," she related, "we tried to organize a *favela* [slum], and soon after our arrival, some people from the PC do B [Communist Party of Brazil] showed up. Fortunately, the people rejected them, and they did not meet their objectives."

Interestingly, as well, just about one-quarter of the personnel saw manipulation by radical pastoral agents as a significant threat to the CEBs' ecclesial character. One priest, for example, though admitting that "almost all of the groups are instrumentalized by the right and the left," saw clerical manipulation as a much more clear and present danger. Another stated similarly, "The priest has a very dominant role. . . . [although] he doesn't exercise control directly . . . his presence is very strong." Still others referred in passing to their counterparts on the periphery in less diplomatic terms, calling them "red priests" and "ideological zealots."

The consequences of ecclesiastical control

The perceived need on the part of the hierarchy for control over the CEB phenomenon has affected all aspects of group life. Where and when the groups will emerge, the types of activities they will engage in—all of these things are determined, to varying extents, by hierarchical initiative.

At the most basic level, it is very doubtful that the CEBs could thrive in the absence of direct intervention by an activist clergy. This is true not only in São Paulo, as was demonstrated in chapter 2, but all over Brazil.

Bruneau, for example, has provided national-survey data that show that the CEBs in Brazil tend to prosper mainly where pastoral agents of the local Church—in particular, the bishop—are favorable to their presence. Conversely, where the local hierarchy is not disposed to the phenomenon, the groups, Bruneau claims, remain dormant.[10] Similar findings were reported in a 1981 CNBB-sponsored research report. In this study, the authors noted a direct link between CEB activation and institutional planning. "In those regions," stated the report, "where there exists a Joint Pastoral Plan in which the [base] community line is defined as a priority task, the CEBs encounter a very favorable climate for their emergence and growth."[11] Finally, a recent work by Baldissera suggests that even where the institutional structure of the Church is rather weak, ecclesiastical initiative remains crucial to the CEBs' survival. In her examination of CEBs in the northeastern dioceses of Crateùs and Fortaleza, she states, "It [is] seen [here] that the CEBs do not emerge spontaneously. Together and each one, there always exists the presence of a bishop, priest, religious or layperson, denominated by the Church hierarchy as a pastoral agent. . . . All of the CEBs are strongly marked by the presence and intervention of these pastoral agents.[12]

The impact of Church control is demonstrated as well in the São Paulo sample. In accordance with results obtained by Bruneau and Baldissera, most of the groups owe their origins to hierarchical initiative. Of the 22 CEBs originally sampled in 1984, 16, or approximately three-quarters, were founded with the assistance of priests or nuns dispatched from the local diocesan office.

The São Paulo sample also reveals considerable ecclesiastical control in day-to-day operations. To begin with, the institutional Church has gone to considerable lengths to ensure that the doors of inter-CEB and Church-CEB communication remain open, principally by encouraging engagement in cooperative ventures and initiatives. For example, in 1984, nearly three-quarters of the groups maintained regular contact with the local parish and participated in its activities. By 1988, this figure had increased to nearly 100 percent. Similarly, the percentage of CEBs sending representatives to Church-sponsored CEB meetings or conferences up to the national level increased from slightly over half to 60 percent.[13]

Second, conformity to Church teaching and practice is maintained in the CEBs through the distribution of specially prepared liturgical pamphlets and other discussion materials, which are in wide use throughout São Paulo. Such materials do vary in political orientation, without question. The liturgical guide *O Domingo*, for instance, tends to avoid political commentary, whereas *Todos irmãos* offers regular opportunity for member debate on current social and political issues. Nevertheless, both call for adherence to the traditional format of the Mass while at the same time reinforcing CEB members' allegiance to both the institution and the members of its hierarchy.

Third, and perhaps most important, elements of institutional control over specific group activities in the devotional and political spheres are evident in many groups. For the most part, such control is exercised through the actions of the pastoral agents who accompany the CEBs.

According to the liberationist view, Church-based activists from outside the CEBs (who are most often recruited from the ranks of the middle class) act as mere advisers, helping only to guide the people's own emergent consciousness. Borrowing a term from the Italian neo-Marxist Antonio Gramsci, Clodovis Boff, for example, has described such individuals as "organic intellectuals," who aid—but do not directly excite—the activist potential of the popular will in specific sociohistorical contexts.[14] This approach to the pastoral agents' role has also been lent further credibility in recent works by North American students of the Brazilian Church such as Adriance.[15]

In the São Paulo sample, however, the involvement of individual pastoral agents assumes quite different and certainly more direct proportions. In fact, the sample data collected in both 1984 and 1988 reveal a definite association between the continued presence of pastoral agents and various aspects of group activity.

The precise nature of this relationship is best shown when the various group types defined in chapter 3 are reexamined in light of the quality of the pastoral agent's presence in each. In essence, this "quality of presence" takes on a variety of forms, depending on the political orientation of pastoral agents and the degree to which they spend time in individual CEBs. Politically speaking, first of all, there are priests and nuns who generally uphold the Church's "option for the poor" and the political role of the CEBs, and other religious personnel who do not. Similarly, there is variation in the willingness of pastoral agents to directly accompany the CEBs in a leadership capacity.

What the data from 1984 and 1988 reveal is a marked tendency for group type to correlate with the presence or absence of progressive Church representatives active in group leadership. For example, in 1984, politically active pastoral agents were all but nonexistent in the more elementary kinds of CEBs. Of the 15 groups in this category (Types I to IV, inclusive), only 1 possessed a progressive pastoral agent on an ongoing basis. By contrast, in the more advanced CEBs (Types V and VI), such individuals were rarely absent. Of the 7 most developed groups, 5 were regularly accompanied by appropriately oriented priests or nuns.

Four years later, the pattern of pastoral agents' involvement had changed considerably, but the importance of their presence or absence remained obvious. By 1988, most of the pastoral agents accompanying the more advanced groups had been reassigned to new duties elsewhere in São Paulo, or even outside the archdiocese. As a result, these groups were engaging far less frequently in more politically and/or organizationally complex undertakings. This hiatus in activation, induced for the most part by hierarchical whim, has had serious consequences for the groups involved, and will be discussed in more detail in chapter 8.

The pastoral agent's presence and function thus defined—it should be stated in closing this discussion—is not necessarily viewed passively by group members themselves. To be sure, the agent's involvement in the group is highly valued. This is true not only because of the material or organizational assistance he or she can offer, but also because of the agent's spiritual significance. Nevertheless, many group members often resent the pastoral agent's efforts to control the CEB's political and religious agendas. In some CEBs, for example, group members have been discouraged by local agents from actively participating in political parties—even from inviting political candidates to address group meetings. Similarly, discussions of sexual matters, such as birth control and premarital sex, have been curtailed by representatives of the Church. At the other end of the scale, pastoral agents have attempted to enjoin group members in political discussion and action in areas that are seen as having little relevance to their daily lives. In one case, CEB members were asked to consider and debate relations between white and black persons in Brazil. Some group participants were unclear about what such a discussion should entail and about whether only certain group members should be involved. As one group member proclaimed, half joking, "But who is black and who is white anyway? I'm half and half. [Much laughter.] There are so few whites anyway, if the Negroes form their own group, there won't be anybody left for ours!" Such attempts to structure group discussions about seemingly irrelevant matters only reinforce some group members' perception that their CEB is overly subject to ecclesiastical control.

Conclusion

CEB organization and leadership can take a number of forms. Some CEBs undertake their various functions as a group, in a spirit of democracy. Others might delegate responsibility for activities or leadership to separate teams or councils.

All CEBs, however, operate under the general guidance of the institutional Church. Sometimes control is exercised rather subtly, other times more directly. Either way, the Church can have considerable say over when, how, and where specific CEB activities will be undertaken.

Owing to all these factors, here again, a considerable amount of diversity is revealed in the CEB phenomenon. Nevertheless, there are other sources of potential variation and conflict that remain to be explored.

5
Social
Location
of the
Membership
▬

To this point, the CEBs have been examined primarily as entities with specific attributes. The demographic aspects of the phenomenon remain to be considered. Just exactly who are the people who call themselves CEB members?

As a collectivity, the individuals who have chosen to involve themselves in the groups have a good deal in common, which is clearly revealed in the São Paulo sample. In terms of politico-religious attitudes and behavior, first of all, they would appear to be firmly on the progressive vanguard of both Brazilian society and the Church. In 1984, for example, only about 3 percent of all respondents claimed to support conservative political parties such as the PDS (the party of the ruling military). The single most favored political force was the PT (Workers' Party), which appealed to some 30 percent of CEB members. Similarly, only about 15 percent of respondents expressed confidence in the politicians of the day to defend their interests, whereas labor unions were believed by 60 percent to do so. As for their Church, the membership placed a good deal of faith in the "option for the poor." Though in 1984 only about 21 percent chose to describe Jesus Christ as a "liberator" of the oppressed, well over 80 percent expressed confidence in the Church's ability to defend the interests of people like themselves and to resolve social injustice generally.

The São Paulo CEB members were also frequent churchgoers, with over 75 percent attending mass at least once a week. In addition, well over 80 percent of group participants prayed regularly to God.

CEB members were in agreement, as well, about why they joined the CEBs. Most stated that they had been invited to participate by friends or members of the clergy. Over 90 percent also cited factors such as a desire to help others and the need for human contact as reasons for joining.

Although CEB members do thus share a number of attitudinal and behavioral traits, the question of where, precisely, they are located within the social structure of Brazil is somewhat more complex. The conventional wisdom, as expressed at least by liberation theology, has portrayed the CEBs as associations of the poor—unemployed and underemployed workers, impoverished women, and disenfranchised youth. Increasingly, however, as more and more social-scientific studies of the CEBs appear, another vision of the CEBs is emerging that stresses the existence of a much more socially heterogeneous membership.

This latter view of CEB participation is supported by the data from the São Paulo groups. The sample reveals a CEB phenomenon that is attracting people from all walks of life—young and old, male and female, rich and poor—albeit to varying extents.

Membership and age

One of the most important characteristics that divides any population in terms of attitudes and behavior is age. As both common sense and the social-scientific literature have suggested, young and old are easily distinguished by level of idealism and commitment to social causes.[1]

When applied to the CEBs, such wisdom would suggest that groups of such obvious political significance should disproportionately attract the young—people ready, willing, and able to change the world—as opposed to older individuals, who have often become more complacent about day-to-day injustices.

In the case of the São Paulo CEBs, however, this is not the case. In fact, the age distribution in the membership is fairly balanced, with the largest number of members in the middle years of life. In 1984, about 33 percent of the sample were under age 30, as compared with 42 percent of respondents in the 30-to-49 age group. The rest, approximately 25 percent, were age 50 and over. In those CEBs whose membership was resurveyed in 1988, the distribution was somewhat similar, although there were fewer members age 50 and over. Thirty-six percent of respondents reported ages up to 30, 48 percent fell into the 30-to-49 age group, and just 14 percent had passed the 50-year mark.

Within the leadership structure, the age distribution in the São Paulo sample was somewhat more skewed, with a slight overrepresentation of older, ostensibly more mature members. Whereas, in 1984, participants over 30 represented two-thirds of all group members, they constituted 77 percent of the leadership. Similarly, in 1988, 73 percent of group leaders and conselho members were over 30, yet they represented just 64 percent of all CEB participants surveyed.

All of this is not to say, of course, that the CEBs somehow depreciate the involvement of young people. If anything, the opposite is true. In most groups, in fact, finding ways to attract new and younger members has become a full-time occupation. Some CEBs even offer special activities of interest to young people, such as parties and dances, and others have attempted to form youth groups.

Unfortunately, however, the CEBs have met only with rather uneven success in this regard. As many group leaders pointed out, effective youth-recruitment campaigns do manage to bring in young people in fairly large numbers, but soon enough they seem to drift away.

The most salient evidence for this tendency is found in the extremely high turnover rate characteristic of many groups. In 1988, for example, about 40 percent of the CEB participants surveyed had joined their group during the previous four years. Yet there was no accompanying increase in group size. If anything, the groups involved had decreased in size since they were first examined in 1984.

Member turnover, especially that involving young people, is seen by many as being directly related to the contradictions to which the Church's "option for the poor" has given rise. As a number of CEB directors explained, many young people are attracted to the CEBs because they see in them an opportunity to live their faith in their way and to participate in the social-reform process. Before too long, however, they realize that political involvement comes with strings attached. Fighting for streetlights and sewers may be seen by Church authorities as worthy activities, but discussing issues of intense interest to youth, such as birth control and premarital sex, is not. As a result, young people tend to feel constrained by ecclesiastical control and, hence, move on to new and less restrictive forms of political involvement.

Gender

Whereas some degree of alienation may be felt by youth—thus limiting higher levels of participation—this is certainly not the case among women. Indeed, the CEBs have traditionally been strongly identified as places where women can work alongside men as equal partners in the struggle for social justice.

Nevertheless, the precise nature of the feminine presence in the CEBs has been the topic of considerable discussion in recent years. Some, especially those within the Church, are extremely optimistic about women's role in the groups and the opportunities they have been afforded as a result of CEB membership. Eduardo Hoornaert, for example, has pointed to the very strong sense of empowerment that the CEBs have offered women, who participate freely and equally with men in the groups' activities and internal decision-making process.[2] Similarly, Leonardo Boff has stated that in "the basic Christian communities, especially, a very important space for the liberation of women is being created. This is not so much because there they deal with the theme of women's liberation, but rather because over half of the coordinators of the communities are women. In all the basic communities, it's the women who are most engaged in work."[3] Finally, Shulamit Goldsmit and Ernest S. Sweeney have held that "as a result of participation in authority as well as in labor of the community, women have become active agents of social change instead of remaining merely passive instruments in a historic process."[4]

Others, though, have taken issue with such glowing reports about sexual equality, albeit for radically different reasons. On the one hand, some have suggested that women's participation in the CEBs is a reflection more of traditionalism than of innovation. If women are indeed active within the CEBs and their leadership, they argue, this is merely because of their time-honored role in Latin American Catholicism, which has customarily been described as the religion of women and children.[5] On the other hand, critics such as Sonia Alvarez have suggested that although the Church may have "empowered women as citizens," it has still largely failed to accept or adequately "cope with women's empowerment as women." Moreover, Alvarez states, "the basic Christian communities are hardly laboratories of women's liberation." In fact, "[t]hough over 80 percent of the membership in CEBs . . . is composed of women, they are seldom found in positions of authority. . . . Moreover, the Church often replicates the society's sexual division of political labor, creating 'separate and unequal' mothers' clubs and housewives' associations which reinforce traditional gender role expectations."[6] A similar criticism has been that women in the CEBs are still subject to certain restrictions to which men are not. For example, both J. B. Libânio and Oliveira have observed that during the National CEB

Encounter at Itaici in 1981, there were many more men in attendance than women.[7] This was attributable, claims Libânio, to the fact that some men would not allow their wives to travel unescorted to the conference.

To at least some extent, the situation of women in the São Paulo CEBs confirms the rather bleak picture of feminine participation presented by Alvarez and others. First, although women are actively present in the CEBs, their concerns are not necessarily at the forefront of group discussion and action. Women's issues per se, for example, were rarely discussed in the sample CEBs during the period of the research. In addition, only one of the CEBs had a regularly functioning women's group expressly designed to debate matters of importance to female group members. Second, differences in the level of respect accorded men and women religious and lay leaders in the CEBs were also evident. Many group members considered the presence of nuns in group activities, for instance, to be far less important than that of priests. The same held true for male and female lay ministers. As one female CEB member explained, attendance rates at local celebrações could be easily predicted by the gender of the celebrant. "If the people come to the celebration and see only lay ministers," she stated, "[many] go home; and if the lay minister is a woman—forget it!"

On a brighter note, though, there is still much evidence from the São Paulo sample to suggest that the groups are, in at least some key respects, providing opportunities for women to work alongside men as equal partners. To begin with, it is important to note that women did make up approximately 60 percent of the total CEB membership surveyed in both 1984 and 1988 and, thus, in terms of sheer numbers, maintained a noteworthy presence. Contrary to Alvarez's claims, moreover, they were not excluded from leadership. Rather, women were an integral part of the governing body in most groups. In 1984, 63 percent of governing council, or conselho, members were women. In the groups studied in 1988, the figure was 46 percent. In addition, within those groups with no conselho, for both years, women were just as likely as men to be in positions of ultimate authority.

Certainly, women do face certain peculiar difficulties. Yet, the challenges a male-dominated Church places in their path can be, and more than occasionally are, overcome. And when women are successful, they provide role models and, hence, impetus for others to follow in their wake.

In the São Paulo sample, there are numerous examples of women who have both been empowered and empowered others, even in the face of innumerable obstacles. One such example is Maria Ferreira dos Santos, the leader of an activist CEB on the eastern periphery of the archdiocese.[8]

Born in 1933 in the interior of São Paulo state, Maria is an average *dona de casa* (housewife) who lives with her husband and two children in a small but comfortable home on one of the few paved streets in her neighborhood. She is not a radical in the political sense, yet, in many ways, she is an ideal candidate for CEB leadership. Unlike most of her friends and acquaintances, Maria has a primary-school education, and has gained valuable organizational experience in the working world as both a salesperson and a dressmaker. In addition, she maintains a modest income from savings and from room and board contributed by her children and, thus, is relatively free to engage full-time in CEB promotion.

Maria first began her involvement with the CEBs in 1983, when she joined a small group situated near her house. It was only a matter of weeks, however, before she was drafted into the governing council and began, of her own accord, a campaign to breathe much-needed new life into the CEB.

To begin with, Maria involved the group, for the first time, in the community-action projects, and was instrumental in the construction of a new community center. She also initiated two new discussion groups in the CEB—one for young people and the other for women—and became involved with a number of already-established activities and teams.

Right from the start, Maria met with various difficulties. Among other group leaders, for one thing, her calls for revitalization fell on deaf ears, leaving much of the responsibility for running the CEB on Maria's shoulders alone.

Perhaps the major impediment to progress, though, has been the Church itself, in the form of the local priest. Whereas Maria prizes openness and discussion, the priest, by his own admission, has worked hard to shield the CEB from what he terms "undesirable" or "harmful" influences. "I don't allow the comunidade to be used," he has warned Maria, "for specific ends, be they political or personal." His efforts in this regard have had a debilitating effect on Maria's work with women and young people. Quite often, those involved in the discussion groups she established for both feel constrained and limited by the traditional Church line that the priest has insisted on. Constantly they are reminded that matters of intense interest to them, including sexual behavior, birth control, and abortion, are not open to full examination.

In response to the apathy of the laity and the authoritarianism of the Church, Maria has been active on a number of fronts. Not only has she diligently sought out and cultivated potential group leaders, she has also begun to criticize the actions of the priest openly, and has encouraged others to do likewise. "The priest," she has stated, "is a man equal to all others. He is like us. He is nothing special."

To a marked extent, these efforts have paid off. The sleepy CEB she joined several years earlier had at least 40 members by 1988—most of them women—and is now engaged in a range of activities in the social-justice sphere. As for the priest, he has moved on to new duties far from São Paulo.

What her success with the CEB indicates, in the final analysis, is that Maria and women like her are at the very least being provided with opportunities to take up leadership roles in both the Church and society. Certainly, the CEBs do not offer women total freedom to fulfill all their aspirations and achieve their full potential. But for those who are determined and persistent, much more can be accomplished than many feminist observers would admit.

Social class

Just as the CEBs, in some measure at least, have opened up opportunities for women to work alongside men, so too, students of the groups have noted, are they helping the poor and oppressed to come to grips with a world dominated by the rich and powerful. In fact, much of the literature has held that the groups, by definition, are a lower-class phenomenon.

To say that the CEBs are exclusively or even primarily lower-class, however, obscures reality in two fundamental respects. To begin with, it suggests that the CEBs proliferate evenly throughout all sectors of the poor. Yet, this is clearly not the case. In actuality, they tend to find most fertile ground among the working poor—the working classes—as opposed to the poorest of the poor. They tend to grow, in other words, among those who are relatively, as opposed to absolutely, deprived. Among the former, it would seem, there is a greater appreciation of the kinds of spiritual and, especially, material benefits that the CEBs can offer (through the community-action projects). Among the latter, group life, where it exists at all, is extremely fragile. This is because, as authors such as Barreiro and Ireland have pointed out, those who are absolutely deprived have frequently lost all hope of ever removing themselves from their disadvantaged situation.[9] Another factor inhibiting group activation among the very poor may be the fact that they see little permanence in their present state of ill fortune and expect to resolve their predicament soon and definitively on their own.

Second, the assumption of a lower-class CEB phenomenon excludes the possibility of CEB growth among more affluent Catholics. To the extent that their existence is admitted at all, groups of the middle or even upper classes are viewed as devotional entities and as lacking a worldly commitment to equality and social justice. Moreover, in their supposed pursuit of more traditional ends, such groups are often seen as essentially misguided. For a CEB to pursue purely religious ends, Cardinal Arns, for example, has stated, "and to lay aside its political dimensions, reducing them to mere practices of prayer, reflection, and worship, without a consequent organized action in favor of life, is to distort what the Sacred Scriptures mean, on the whole, by religious."[10] One of Cardinal Arns's most outspoken former auxiliary bishops, Dom Angélico Bernardino of São Miguel region, has taken an even harder line and has refused to discuss the possibility of CEBs originating outside of the lower classes. When asked, for instance, if groups among the more affluent in his region could be considered authentic (that is, oriented toward social change), he angrily retorted, "I am not worried about whether or not they are real. I am only worried about our CEBs [of the poor, who are] exploited by the politicians and the multinationals."[11]

Yet, in many ways, the CEBs are just as "real" (to borrow Dom Angélico's term) for the more affluent as they are for the lower classes. As Bruneau, in his 1982 study of Brazilian CEBs, concluded, the CEBs can and do thrive in all social classes, in conformity with the Church's general commitment to the cause of social justice.[12]

Within the São Paulo archdiocese as a whole, there is unmistakable evidence for such a claim. Although CEBs of the lower classes are certainly in the majority in the archdiocese, as was shown in the quantitative examination of CEB distribution undertaken in chapter 2, the groups are clearly present as well in more affluent neighborhoods throughout the region.

An examination of the background characteristics of group members from the São Paulo CEB sample reveals similar diversity in terms of class. In the comprehensive survey of CEB participants conducted in 1984, for example, measures of income, education, and occupation all varied widely.[13] With respect to income, first of all, about 20 percent of respondents earned less than 2 minimum salaries,[14] 31 percent earned between 2 and 5, 19 percent took home between 5 and 10, and 16 percent were paid in excess

Table 4. Social Class Indicators of CEB Members, 1984
(in Percentages)

Class indicator	Lower-class (n=151)	Middle-class (n=124)
Education, beyond secondary level	25	52*
Profession, white-collar (nonclerical)	28	79*
Earnings over 5 MS	37	66*

*Differences between member types are significant at or below the .05 level.

of 10.[15] As for education, approximately 27 percent had had little or no primary schooling, 22 percent had finished elementary school, 22 percent had had at least some high school education, and 26 percent had undertaken some form of postsecondary training. Finally, about half the sample were employed in what might be termed white-collar (nonclerical) occupations, and the remainder worked as wage laborers in the service and industrial sectors.

Nevertheless, recalling the criticism of the São Paulo hierarchy, the question naturally arises of whether the CEBs that include these individuals of such diverse class backgrounds really have anything in common. In fact, despite a number of salient differences, the sample demonstrates that CEBs formed in a variety of social-class settings are surprisingly similar in both organization and objectives.

This can be demonstrated quite effectively by comparing, in certain key respects, groups from the sample of more affluent, middle-class areas with those from lower-class districts. In 1984, there were 11 CEBs in each category. In 1988, there were 10.

As Table 4 shows, the membership within these two types of groups in 1984 was not homogenous in terms of class. Just as there are CEBs of the rich and the poor, so too are there more and less affluent participants present in individual groups. Nevertheless, in each class indicator, the difference between members in the two CEB categories is both strong and significant.

Table 5 profiles the activities regularly offered by the lower- and middle-class CEBs described above for both 1984 and 1988. In 1984, the two types of CEBs exhibited patterns of activity preferences that were strikingly similar. In the case of traditional activities, to begin with, the middle-class CEBs in the sample were, on balance, no more likely than their lower-class counterparts to engage in functions such as Bible study or the planning of festive occasions. The only exception here was charity work, which is

Table 5. Activity Profile of Lower- and Middle-Class CEBS, 1984 and 1988

Activity	1984 (No. CEBS participating)		1988 (No. CEBS participating)	
	Lower (n=11)	Middle (n=11)	Lower (n=10)	Middle (n=10)
Traditional activities:				
Charity work	4	7	8	6
Bible study	5	6	9	9
Religious festive days	6	5	8	5
Innovative activities:				
Local celebrações	8	4*	8	4*
Preparation of celebrações	7	3*	7	4
Preparation for other sacraments	5	2	7	4
Reflection and discussion	10	9	8	10
Consciousness raising	5	3	5	4
Community action	6	4	8	3*

*Differences between group type during year in question are significant at or below the
.10 level.

clearly an activity that has historically attracted more affluent Catholics who are, of course, also the best equipped to undertake it.

In the sphere of innovative functions, again in 1984, more politically oriented activities such as biblical reflection, consciousness raising, and the community-action projects were only marginally (and statistically nonsignificantly) less popular in the more affluent CEBs than in those of the poor. The greatest divergencies appeared in more innovative religious functions, including the celebrações and the preparation of other sacraments. These differences, however, likely have little to do with class. Rather, they can be attributed to the varying quality of Church infrastructure and the availability of funding in the archdiocese. In the first place, the lower-class CEBS are located, for the most part, in sprawling semi-urban districts, where parishes are enormous and the distance to the local church great. Hence, there is an increased need here for local services, which are not lacking in urban middle-class areas, where parishes are comparatively small and churches abound. Second, the Church in São Paulo has actively encouraged and provided funds for the construction of local community centers in poor areas, but has made no such provision for more affluent CEB members.

By 1988, the comparison of activity offerings for both middle- and

Table 6. Organizational Features and Institutional Linkages
of Lower- and Middle-Class CEBs, 1984 and 1988

	1984		1988	
Feature or linkage	Lower (n=11)	Middle (n=11)	Lower (n=10)	Middle (n=10)
Meet weekly	4	5	2	4
Lay ministers active	4	3	8	5
Subgroups or teams	7	4	7	4
Conselho	7	5	6	5
Parish group contact	9	8	10	10
Attend CEB encounters	6	6	10	10
Pastoral agents involved in group formation	7	9	6	8
Pastoral agents presently active in leadership	6	2*	5	6

*Differences between group type during year in question are significant at or below the .10 level.

lower-class CEBs had shifted slightly, but certainly not in the direction of greater overall dissimilarity. If anything, the two types of CEBs appeared to be moving closer together in terms of functional preferences. As Table 5 reveals, more traditional activities—formerly favored somewhat disproportionately by the middle-class groups—had become more attractive to the lower-class CEBs, whereas the more affluent groups were increasingly likely to be involved in the more innovative functions they had previously avoided. Only the community-action projects appear to have been established more firmly as a lower-class function.

Aside from matters related to activity preferences, middle- and lower-class CEBs shared, in both 1984 and 1988, a good deal in organizational structure and institutional linkages. As Table 6 shows, the middle- and lower-class CEBs were almost equally likely to possess a conselho, maintain contact with other parish groups, attend CEB encounters, and—by 1988 at least—count on the presence of active pastoral agents. The only categories showing notable differences involved meeting times and the presence of lay ministers and functional subgroups. If the middle-class CEBs met more frequently, however, and possessed fewer teams, or subgroups, it was largely a function of their smaller size, as opposed to the class origin of their members. Similarly, there is a smaller need for lay ministers in the more affluent groups because, as was explained earlier, they are often located quite near the parish church and can more freely obtain the services of the local priest.

A number of broad similarities between and among CEB members in terms of class are thus readily apparent. In the final analysis, however, general affinities between the middle- and lower-class group types should not be overstated. To overemphasize these affinities would be equally erroneous as to insist upon the image of an exclusively lower-class CEB phenomenon.

What must be pointed out is that in at least some respects, CEBs operating in different class settings can be and often are quite distinctly dissimilar. Usually, such differences are traced to the nature of the political activities that are undertaken by CEBs in poor and wealthy areas respectively.

As was revealed previously, the lower-class CEBs in the sample were generally more likely to be engaged in one particular form of political activity—the community-action projects—than were those in wealthier areas. This in itself is significant. Yet, it is not so much the quantity of this involvement in political action that distinguishes the CEBs of the poor from their more affluent counterparts.

In chapter 3, a number of CEB types were defined, according to the groups' activities and the frequency with which they were undertaken. These range from the least religiously and politically innovative (Types I, II, and III) to the most advanced, or mature, CEBs (Types IV, V, and VI).

When these types are broken down by social class, a fairly obvious relationship emerges. Though both lower- and middle-class CEBs are equally capable of adopting a variety of forms, the most innovative groups of either class tend to cluster in certain categories. The middle-class CEBs, for their part, are not found beyond Type V, with the bulk at the lower end in the politically oriented miniparish category (Type IV). The lower-class groups, by contrast, are found exclusively in the classical, or ideal-typical, (Type VI) CEB category.

The factors that distinguish these two categories (Type IV from Type VI), and thus the more advanced middle-class CEBs from the lower-class groups, are the quality and intensity of the political activity in which they are involved. CEBs in both group types may engage in consciousness raising and community action, but the lower-class groups of the ideal-typical, or classical, type are much more effective in bringing about social change, as will be argued subsequently.

Conclusion

As a social phenomenon, the CEBs draw upon a variety of individuals from very diverse backgrounds. Within the groups, opportunities for expression and action are provided to all with the ability and the desire to become involved. This includes people of either sex and every age.

To a considerable extent, the groups are also attractive to individuals of different social-class backgrounds. Moreover, generally speaking, CEB members from rich and poor neighborhoods exhibit similar levels of engagement in and commitment to activities with politico-religious ends. Nevertheless, it must be noted that important differences do exist between groups operating in different class milieus—differences related to the quality and intensity of political activity that members undertake.

6
A Case Study of the Comunidades Santa Heléna and São José
—

To this point, a general portrait of the CEB phenomenon has been traced with specific reference to the diverse activities of the groups and the attitudes, behavior, and characteristics of their membership. What is still missing, though, is a more detailed sketch of just what any given CEB actually is and does.

The following discussion provides a more comprehensive picture of CEB life in Brazil by focusing on the basic structure and thrust of two of the more mature groups from the São Paulo sample. For purposes of comparison and contrast, these CEBs were selected because they are located at opposite ends of the archdiocese, both geographically and socially.[1]

The first of these, the Comunidade Santa Heléna, is representative of the predominantly middle-class, Type IV CEB category (described in chapter 3), and is situated in a relatively affluent neighborhood near the city center. The second, the Comunidade São José, is a rather average Type VI CEB, and is in a working-class district on the southern periphery of São Paulo. Although the two groups have much in common, as will be shown, there are a number of subtle and not so subtle differences between them in both internal organization and action. These differences, for the most part, are directly related to the class position of group members.

Comunidade Santa Heléna
Origins. The Comunidade Santa Heléna forms part of the Nossa Senhora Aparecida parish, one of the oldest and most prestigious divisions in the eastern episcopal region of São Miguel and, indeed, in all of São Paulo. Nossa Senhora Aparecida is a strictly urban parish, and most of its 20,000 inhabitants are of middle- to lower middle-class origin. About 44 percent

of residents in the general area earn from 5 to 12 minimum salaries, and another 11 percent take home in excess of 12 minimum salaries.[2]

Since 1974, the parish has been administered by Pe. Cláudio, a 48-year-old Brazilian-born diocesan priest. In some respects, the local pastor does not conform to the image of the typical pastoral agent. He has spent most of his clerical career working in middle-class parishes and consequently has little experience with either the lower classes or the CEBs per se. Nevertheless, Pe. Cláudio is a staunch supporter of the groups and believes that they "are going to change Brazilian society," insofar as they represent "the power of the little guy."

To encourage the formation of CEBs in his parish, the priest has taken action over the years on a number of fronts. For example, he has regularly engaged in what he terms *propaganda massista* (verbal encouragement through the Mass), and visits with individual lay groups as much as possible. More concretely, he also attempted, in 1978, to artificially create additional CEBs by subdividing the parish into separate sectors, or zones. In each of these zones, lay groups were subsequently formed and given a degree of autonomy to pursue goals relevant to the "option for the poor."

One of the most successful of these groups is the Comunidade Santa Heléna, which is situated in a rather isolated neighborhood at the southern end of the parish. In 1984, the CEB counted a total of about 20 to 30 participants (the same number was recorded in 1988); some 40 percent of these were under 29 years of age, and another 40 percent were over 50. As in many CEBs, most, moreover, were women (61 percent).

Goals and activities. In the range of activities that it undertakes, the Comunidade Santa Heléna is very typical of the politically oriented mini-parish CEBs of the middle classes. Whereas it tends to concentrate primarily on more traditional and innovative devotional and religious functions, it also frequently engages in various forms of political action.

In the religious sphere, members perform a variety of tasks. They prepare weekly celebrações and occasional baptisms, participate in Bible study and reflection, offer religious instruction to the young and charity to the poor, and plan festivals to mark holy days.

The political activities offered are basically of two types. Consciousness raising, first of all, is frequently practiced, and reportedly intensifies as political themes suggest themselves in discussion materials or everyday life. During extensive flooding in 1983, for example, members considered the plight of local favelados and others who had been adversely affected. The comunidade also engages in community-action projects. For instance,

CEB participants have formed a kind of community watch, and keep one another informed of suspicious occurrences and the presence of strangers in the neighborhood. They have even set up an alarm system to warn of impending danger. Much more important, however, the CEB engages from time to time in joint-labor projects known as *mutirões*. Sometimes these are undertaken in the members' own interests. For example, when some of their own homes were flooded in 1983, the membership pitched in to buy materials and repair the damage. For the most part, though, the mutirões are directed toward helping others—favelados or CEB members in poorer areas of the parish or the region—to rebuild after calamities, or to find food, clothing, and/or medicine.

Organizational structure. To support its various functions, the comunidade maintains a highly evolved organizational structure. Although CEB members do not meet collectively outside of religious services, there are many subgroups, or teams, that come together regularly to discuss and carry out various activities. Such teams currently exist for young people, religious instruction, fund-raising, liturgy preparation, baptismal preparation, festival-day planning, and charity. Normally, these convene in the group's community center, a rather impressive structure that was built by the members (through the mutirões) on land owned by the central curia.

In charge of the group is a central directorate, or conselho. The CEB possesses no lay ministers, so this inner circle consists exclusively of the leaders of the CEB's various teams, plus a treasurer and central coordinator, who are elected at large from the membership.

Conselho meetings, which occur once a month, serve both a religious and a secular purpose. During encounters, time is allowed not only for team progress and financial reports, but for prayer, song, and reflection as well. This last activity is usually undertaken without special materials and is based entirely on readings from the Bible. At the close of each meeting, coffee and biscuits are served, and members chat amicably among themselves for an hour or so before going home.

Institutional relations. As pointed out earlier, the Comunidade Santa Heléna is essentially the creation of the parish pastor, Pe. Cláudio. Nevertheless, on a day-to-day basis it operates under extremely weak clerical control. While Pe. Cláudio is generally considered to be the CEB's spiritual director, decisions regarding group activities, including the more political of these, are left exclusively to the conselho. The conselho is responsible merely for informing the priest regularly of any changes in the structural direction of the group.

Beyond the parish, the comunidade has formed a number of ties. Aside from working regularly with other CEBs and parish lay groups on Church-based projects, as well as on the mutirões, the group has been represented at institutionally sponsored CEB-related encounters up to the state level.

Comunidade São José

Though representative of the Type VI CEBs, the second group to be examined, the Comunidade São José, would appear to share a good deal with Santa Heléna in terms of activities undertaken and organizational form. Still and all, though, there are some very important differences between the two groups, mostly related to the fact that the functions undertaken by the poorer CEB are much more closely tied to the daily lives and needs of the membership.

Origins. The Comunidade São José is situated on the southern periphery of São Paulo in the parish of São Gabriel. The parish itself has approximately 90 thousand inhabitants. Most of these are poor, earning less—and in some cases much less—than five minimum salaries.

For a number of years, the parish has been administered by a team of religious priests—members of the Congregação dos Missionários Oblatos da Maria Imaculada (OMI)—who live together in a small, rustic dwelling not unlike most others in the area. In charge of the group is Pe. Marcos, a 47-year-old American who has been working in São Gabriel since 1974.

Like Pe. Cláudio of Santa Heléna, Pe. Marcos is a committed CEB supporter, and he shares the enthusiasm for the groups expressed by his archbishop, Cardinal Arns. He refuses, for example, to see the groups' political role as separate from their religious purpose, and is actively involved in CEB formation and development.

In quantitative terms, at least, this commitment to the CEBs has appeared to pay off. In 1988, there were reported to be 17 CEBs operating in the parish of São Gabriel, nearly all of which were formed after the priest's arrival.

One of the oldest of these CEBs is the Comunidade São José. This group has been in existence since 1967, and by 1988 had approximately 20 to 25 regular members. Most of these (70 percent) were members of low-income families earning less than five minimum salaries. The majority (60 percent), moreover, were over 40 years of age, and some 70 percent were female.

Goals and activities. São José was originally formed by a group of concerned parents who wished to provide local religious-instruction classes for their children. Since its inception, however, the CEB has developed a number of additional functions, some of a devotional and others of a more political nature. In terms of its aims and the complexity of the tasks it undertakes, the CEB is, in fact, one of the most evolved in the parish.

Regarding the more religious activities, the comunidade appears little different from Santa Heléna. Aside from providing religious instruction, for example, members prepare and offer weekly religious services, or celebrações, preparation for parents of candidates for baptism, intensive Bible study, and biblical reflection. In addition, CEB participants frequently offer charitable support to individual families as the needs arise, and often plan socials and religious festivals for simple diversion or profit.

In terms of political functions, the CEB is involved in both consciousness raising and the community-action projects, just as is the Comunidade Santa Heléna. Nevertheless, these activities are undertaken in São José with a sense of importance and urgency not witnessed in the more advanced middle-class CEBs. Consciousness raising, for example, is not simply an opportunity to discuss the plight of the unfortunate. Rather, it usually involves examination and debate of political and social issues of direct interest to the poor themselves, such as workers' rights, political-party platforms, police violence, and race and gender discrimination. Similarly, the community-action projects, known locally as revindicações, are neither assistance-oriented nor seasonal, as tends to be the case in many more affluent CEBs. Instead, these are long-term projects reflecting specific goals, and are aimed exclusively at improving the quality of life for group members and their neighbors.

The group's first such project was launched in 1976, shortly after Pe. Marcos's arrival in the parish, and was aimed at legalizing the status of local land plots that had been transferred to their present owners without benefit of title. This accomplished, the CEB then circulated petitions throughout the neighborhood in a bid to obtain running water and sewers. A short time later, both of these services were installed. In 1982, the CEB demanded and obtained streetlights, and in 1983 secured a pedestrian overpass across a busy highway nearby. Since 1984, CEB members have fought for and obtained limited street paving and improved bus service, and have initiated actions to secure a local day-care center and a municipal health post.

Organizational structure. As in the Comunidade Santa Heléna, all of the activities offered by São José are carried out within specific teams, or study circles. Thus, there are separate subgroups for religious instruction, Bible study, reflection, liturgy preparation, and baptismal preparation, and for young people in general, most of which meet weekly. There are also general meetings of all group members every two weeks or so. During these encounters, members discuss the progress of individual subgroups, or other matters of importance as they arise. Sometimes, as well, the meetings provide an opportunity for consciousness raising.

Religious services, or celebrações, are held each Sunday in the community hall, which was constructed by the CEB members. These are presided over by either Pe. Marcos or the CEB's two lay ministers, and are open to all area residents. Aside from their religious function, the celebrações, like the general-membership meetings, are frequently oriented toward political discussion. This is usually undertaken by the priest or lay minister after the homily, and is centered around material contained in liturgical pamphlets or special booklets sent from the regional or central curia.

Leadership in the Comunidade São José is exercised in much the same way as it is in Santa Heléna. The governing body, or conselho, consists of some six members and meets twice monthly to deal with matters related to the day-to-day operation of the CEB and its various teams, or subgroups. In addition, all group-related expenditures—for writing materials, travel, liturgical and discussion aids, community-center maintenance, and so forth—are tracked and accounted for.

Without question, however, its primary concern, unlike that of its middle-class counterpart, are the community-action projects, or revindicações. In São José, these actions are both initiated and closely monitored by the conselho directly. The process itself usually involves calling the membership together to discuss the problem at hand, and then drawing up petitions and circulating them throughout the neighborhood. Signed petitions are later taken to the appropriate city officials, and meetings subsequently arranged between CEB and government representatives until the group's demands are met.

Institutional relations. Unlike the Comunidade Santa Heléna, São José is both closely tied to and dependent on ecclesial authority. Although the CEB was essentially lay-initiated, it has long operated under the watchful eye of the parish pastor, Pe. Marcos, who is also a prominent member of the group's central directorate.

Though such intense ecclesial involvement has certain drawbacks, CEB members generally see it as beneficial. When questioned, lay leaders adamantly asserted that they required Pe. Marcos's guidance and approval, and that the comunidade as a whole would likely not function as it presently does without his presence. One of the CEB's lay ministers, for example, found Pe. Marcos's help indispensible in preparing the celebrações, in spite of the fact that the CEB maintains a liturgy group especially for this purpose. "Without Pe. Marcos," she claimed, "I don't know how the celebrações would turn out. It's really a lot of work, a lot of responsibility, and I can't always count on the others to help me out."

Pe. Marcos is cognizant of his special role in the group and speaks freely of his attempts to orient its members. The priest made specific reference, for example, to certain "threats" to be countered, such as the religious traditionalism engendered by the conservative Roman Catholic Charismatic Renewal Movement. One time, he related, he had been forced to reprimand one of its adherents who was attempting to convince CEB members to abandon their involvement with the revindicações. The potential concentration of power within the group was also mentioned by Pe. Marcos as a major concern—one he claims to deal with by actively promoting frequent changes in the membership of the conselho.

Such interference is justified, stated the priest, because the people are basically in need of guidance in both spiritual and political matters. "People," he explained, "have to be activated for the common good." "You have to have patience," Pe. Marcos warned, however, because "real CEBS are not just created overnight."

In addition to the close relationship it maintains with Pe. Marcos, the Comunidade São José does sometimes act in conjunction with other parish CEBs, especially in carrying out the revindicações. It appears, in fact, to be moving more and more in this direction, for nearly all of the projects carried out after 1984 have been undertaken with some measure of cooperation with neighboring CEBs.

The group also sends representatives beyond the parish to CEB-related conferences. These encounters are sponsored by the hierarchy at the various levels of Church government, and provide an opportunity for CEB members and Church personnel to share experiences, to develop strategies for promoting CEB growth and development, and to exchange views on Church policy.

Conclusion

Although they operate in substantially different social settings and represent different CEB types, the Comunidades Santa Heléna and São José are very similar in many ways. They undertake a similar range of activities, conduct their business in similar fashion, and interact with the institutional Church and various other lay groups and organizations in a like manner.

Nevertheless, there are a number of crucial differences between the two CEBs, especially in political engagement and practice. The middle-class Comunidade Santa Heléna largely restricts its political involvement to discussion of social issues in a generic fashion and to community-based projects and activities that assist others. The political activities of the Comunidade São José, by contrast, are much broader in scope, and reflect a sense of immediacy and direct relevance to the deprived situation of the poor themselves. In addition, this involvement in São José benefits disproportionately from the constant encouragement and active support provided by a pastoral agent strongly committed to the "option for the lower classes."

Such differences, also alluded to in chapter 5, are significant in understanding the ultimate impact of the CEBs in Brazilian society. Indeed, as will be shown in the next chapter, if social change is to occur, it will likely be as a function of actions undertaken in groups such as the Comunidade São José, as opposed to middle-class CEBs, such as Santa Heléna.

7
The
Potential
for Social
Change

—

Given the nature of the CEBs and the quality of group activation that has been described thus far, it can be argued that certainly all CEBs have at least some role to play in transforming Brazilian society—if only in awakening citizens to the need for change. Nevertheless, it is probably the more advanced lower-class groups—the Type VI, or ideal-typical, CEBs—that possess the greatest potential in this regard. After all, as was shown in chapters 5 and 6, they are directly involved in the actual work of change, through intense consciousness raising and, especially, the revindicações.

What remains to be answered, however, is how, precisely, social transformation is effected through the political activity of these groups. An answer to this question requires a much closer examination of the more politically engaged, lower-class CEBs in the São Paulo sample.

Interpretations of the CEBs' role
In general, interpretations of the CEBs' this-worldly role tend to paint the phenomenon with a fairly wide brush, making few, if any, distinctions between types of CEBs and their effectiveness. Moreover, they tend to fill a very wide spectrum, from the extremely cautious to the utopian.

At the one end of the scale, on the left, there is a decided tendency to downplay any influence of the CEBs in social and political matters. For those clinging to the ghost of Marx, the Church and the CEBs remain the "opium of the people"—still a contributing factor, not the solution, to the grave problems facing Brazil and Latin America generally. Some neo-Marxists, it is true, do view religious innovation more sympathetically. But their interpretations are invariably made in the context of the broader class struggle. Thus, whereas groups like the CEBs are recognized as potentially influential, they are still, in essence, considered to be an expression of, and ancillary to, a much wider revolutionary process.[1]

Another, slightly more positive view of the CEBs is not so much a formal theory as a popular belief. This position argues that due to the numerical strength of the groups in Brazil, their primary impact is articulated through the electoral sphere. CEB-member support, it has been suggested, will, over time, benefit left-wing parties such as the Partido dos Trabalhadores (Workers' Party), which will then use their political clout to chart a more just and equitable course for Brazilian society.

Toward the utopian end of the scale, progressive members of the Church hierarchy see a still further reaching CEB impact. Cardinal Arns of São Paulo, for example, a prominent spokesman for this view, sees a major role for the CEBs in Brazilian society—one that springs entirely from their character as Christian organizations. The groups, he maintains, have a strong liberating function, which is both religious and political. Where this liberating function expresses itself most clearly, Dom Paulo claims, is in the CEBs' pursuit of basic reforms. Through activities such as the revindicações, the CEBs "stimulate reflection and the social engagement of their members."[2] Nevertheless, they themselves do not change the world directly. The actual mechanics of political change, states the cardinal, are best left to those organizations that are explicitly designed to operate within the world of politics:

> To the extent that in the base communities there are conditions created for . . . consciousness to grow, they end up politically involved, stemming from the solidarity expressed with the difficulties of the people from which these communities are born. But the political solutions, the strategies of political action, of syndical action, are elaborated in nonecclesial instances, with the unions, the political parties, and the various organizations of the popular movement.[3]

One last perspective to be considered, posited by liberation theology, goes even one step further. In early accounts offered by Barreiro, Betto, and Leonardo Boff, the CEBs, rather than facilitating action elsewhere, are a class-rooted and oriented phenomenon that engages the poor directly in the process of social renewal.[4] Through the practices they develop, especially consciousness raising and involvement in the revindicações, CEB members are seen as adopting a broader sense of social responsibility and sense of mission. In and of themselves, then, the CEBs are the seeds of a new society that, in the words of Frei Betto, will and must be "popular, democratic and socialist."[5]

There is at least some merit in each of the positions on CEB influence described above. Nevertheless, along with a collective propensity to view the CEBS as an undifferentiated mass, all are flawed in some fundamental respect.

Conventional Marxist arguments, for example, have largely underestimated the influence of religious innovation, ostensibly in the interests of ideological purity. That the CEBS represent an autonomous force for change in at least some measure should be clear by this point and is, in fact, strongly upheld by some Catholic authors with Marxist leanings, such as Maduro.

Without question, the electoral-impact model is attractive, and certainly there is some evidence substantiating its claim for the existence of a CEB-PT alliance. In the São Paulo sample, for instance, the left-wing Workers' Party has typically been the favorite among group members. Similarly, at national CEB meetings in Itaici (1981) and Canindé (1983), nearly two-thirds of CEB representatives active in party politics opted for the PT. Galletta has indicated, as well, that of 902 individuals connected with various social-justice initiatives of the Church—a good number of whom would be active in CEBS—nearly 70 percent ran for the PT as candidates in the 1982 general elections.[6] The fact is, however, that in spite of these numbers, it is extremely difficult to show a link between the CEBS and the electoral success of the Workers' Party in Brazil. On the one hand, as was shown in the Introduction, the CEBS represent a relatively small fraction of the Brazilian population and thus lack a presence sufficient to tip the scales in favor of the PT. On the other hand, the PT, until very recently, has scored very few electoral successes in any case. Where advances have been made—particularly in the 1988 municipal elections and the strong showing of party leader Luis Inácio da Silva in the 1989 presidential contest—these are likely as attributable to middle-class voter dissatisfaction with the established parties as to CEB block voting.

The perspective emanating from the Church also lacks empirical backing. Dom Paulo may claim that the CEBS are liberating in the way they prepare their membership for participation in political associations, but this is difficult—if not impossible—to prove in the absence of attitude surveys of CEB members past and present. CEB members' reasons for engaging in secular organizations may have as much to do with alienation from Church teaching as with any CEB-inspired desire to promote liberation.

Similarly, the conception of the CEBS developed by liberationism appears to be based more on wishful thinking than on social-scientific investigation. Moreover, liberationist notions of the CEBS' present and future role are extremely vague. To some extent, accounts appearing after 1986 have attempted to come to grips with both of these criticisms. Libânio, for instance, commenting on the CEBS' national encounter at Trindade, Goiás, in 1986, points to difficulties arising from tensions between official and grass-roots visions of the CEBS' mandate—difficulties that may limit their potential for action.[7] Clodovis Boff also engages in more critical commentary, although he poses his concerns somewhat rhetorically in the form of questions for study and debate. What will the new society look like? he asks. How will the political-party question be resolved? What will the new Church of the CEBS look like?[8] Hoornaert has similarly discussed flaws in earlier, more simplistic visions of the CEBS' this-worldly role. He has written that no longer can sympathetic observers "insist too much on the consistency and irreversibility of this movement," noting, among other things, that (a) bourgeois leadership remains in place in most groups and popular autonomous leadership has yet to emerge, (b) an air of liberal elitism still permeates the CEBS, and (c) relations between the CEBS and voluntary/civil associations remain ambiguous.[9] Whether the discussion of these concerns, as voiced by Hoornaert and others, will ultimately lead to the modification of liberationist thinking on the CEBS remains, however, to be seen.

The enhancement of citizenship

As in all things, the truth about CEB effectiveness in the social and political spheres lies somewhere between the extremes. Certainly, the CEBS do contribute to change—they are capable of transforming Brazilian society and of doing so in more fundamental ways than Marxist or electoral-impact models would allow. Nevertheless, this change is far more subtle, far more indirect than the more optimistic (and especially liberationist) visions of the groups have suggested.

A few of the social-scientific accounts of the CEBS' this-worldly impact appearing since 1988 have certainly provided some clues about what this more subtle contribution to change might be. Ireland, for example, talks about the importance of the CEBS in strengthening the voice of the poor within the traditional structure of Brazilian politics.[10] The CEBS, he argues, can in some respects be seen as intermediate bodies standing between the relative powerless citizenry in Brazil and the all-powerful State. Mainwaring, likewise, has argued that the CEBS may be breaking down elitist patterns in Brazil, thus paving the way for more authentic forms of popular participation in governmental decision making.[11] Finally, Levine, based on research he conducted in Venezuela and Colombia, states that the CEBS may help nurture a more independent, "congregational" style of worship among their members—a kind long seen in the Protestant churches.[12] This new style of faith, he argues, helps undermine traditional religious structures and opens the door to popular action in the secular world among a more confident and articulate laity.

Building on these notions of the CEBs' impact in society and politics, a still more comprehensive, yet focused, account of the relationship between group activation and social change can be constructed. This model, to be offered here, takes as its point of departure not all of the CEBs, as is the case with much previous work, but only the groups predominant among the lower classes—namely, those of Type VI.

In effect, these CEBs can be seen as a kind of "carrier group" in the Weberian sense, much like the Protestant sects of post-Reformation Europe and the early United States. Such groups, as Weber has argued in *The Protestant Ethic* and elsewhere, developed and propagated a new ethic that had a profound effect on economic and political development in the West.[13] Similarly, the more politically engaged, or Type VI, CEBs, through the activities they support, contribute to a new way of being and acting on the part of the Brazilian lower classes.

The principal mechanism for change in these CEBs can be traced to unique benefits accruing from their involvement in direct forms of political struggle—in particular, the revindicações. At the most elementary level, this activity has considerable importance as a vehicle for improving the local quality of life. In conjunction with other lay groups and secular organizations, the more politically advanced CEBs in São Paulo, generally, have literally transformed the face of their neighborhoods. In areas roughly corresponding to the episcopal regions of Santo Amaro and São Miguel (where the Type VI CEBs in the sample are located), 300 streets were paved during 1986 and 1987.[14] Between 1982 and 1986, the number of water connections rose by 25 percent in both areas, and sewer connections increased by 52 percent in Santo Amaro and 148 percent in São Miguel. There were also dramatic changes in the number of health-care facilities, especially in São Miguel. Here, between 1981 and 1986, first-aid centers and walk-in clinics increased by over 200 percent.[15]

By encouraging their members to participate in these projects, the more advanced lower-class CEBs have done more, however, than simply contribute to infrastructural improvement. The fact is that through the revindicações, they are implanting in the poor a sense of empowerment, which in turn contributes to the establishment of citizenship in the broadest sense.

Brazil, as a number of authors have noted, is a society that has traditionally been dominated by elites.[16] Since the European discovery of Brazil in 1500, moreover, relationships between these elites and the masses have been guided by a specific operational code often referred to as patron-clientelism. In accordance with this system, the poor are, in essence, dependents of powerful and paternalistic *patrões* (patrons), to whom allegiance is paid in return for favors and protection. Thus, in the countryside, the peasant has customarily relied on the landowner for the basic tools of production and the necessities of life, and has been expected to serve the *patrão* by providing labor or political support. In the cities, the exchange-of-favor mechanism contributes to a very personalist form of social interchange, both in the workplace and in politics generally. Programs and platforms are often pushed aside as union leaders and politicians attempt to build and maintain support through the dispensation of goods and services to key individuals and groups. For the masses, in both cases, things get accomplished not so much because of what is done but because of who is known and can be relied on to deliver.[17]

What the Type VI CEBs offer the poor is an opportunity to break this net of dependent reciprocity by encouraging their participants to create a world of their own making. In working together with pastoral agents to press local officials for sewers, streetlights, or land reform, they learn that very often the best way to achieve their goals is not by appealing as individuals to omnipotent authorities but by working together for the common good. The poor of the CEBs are developing, in other words, that spirit of "enlightened self-interest" that Alexis de Tocqueville attributed to those proud and simple folk who laid the groundwork for America's political culture in the early 19th century.[18]

In the ideal-typical (Type VI) CEBs in the São Paulo sample, there is ample proof of the existence of this process of empowerment through the exercise of enlightened self-interest. To some extent, it is revealed in members' perceptions of the benefits their groups offer in the sphere of political action. In 1984, for example, 58 percent of respondents from Type VI CEBs, as compared with about half of all CEB participants generally, reported enhanced consciousness of social and political problems as a function of group membership. Significantly, as well, some 60 percent, as opposed to 57 percent overall, stated that their CEB had afforded them an opportunity to resolve the day-to-day difficulties of existence. By 1988, these numbers had jumped dramatically. In that year, 67 percent of Type VI CEB members claimed enhanced social and political consciousness, and 88 percent stated that their group had helped them respond to societal ills.

Additional evidence of the CEBs' citizenship-building function is revealed through the existence of an important anomaly of CEB growth and activation cited in chapter 5: the propensity for the more advanced lower-class CEBs to multiply primarily among the more "affluent" poor, such as the urban working classes on the outskirts of São Paulo—among people, in other words, who in some ways closely resemble Tocqueville's early Americans. These individuals may live in what many would call slum areas, yet they do own their own homes and have thus achieved at least some success in life. They see, moreover, the potential for achieving more, a potential that may be satisfied quite nicely through mutual cooperation in the CEBs. As many CEB participants from the São Paulo sample were quick to point out (often to the dismay of more radical pastoral agents), obtaining running water and garbage pickup not only improves the look and the quality of the neighborhood, but serves as well to increase the value of one's own property!

By contrast with their better-off counterparts, the poorest of the poor (the residents of favelas and inner-city rooming houses, or *pensões*) are rarely the targets of successful church-directed CEB-promotion efforts, because they, for various reasons, have as yet acquired little or no stake in their community. Some simply plan to move on to a better location at any moment, and still others have lost all hope of ever resolving their predicament. Among individuals such as these, collective action as a form of "enlightened self-interest" makes little sense and offers few obvious or immediate benefits.

Problems in effecting change

To the extent that their involvement in the revindicações is sustained, there is every chance, then, that the CEBs may ultimately contribute to the emergence of a responsible, involved citizenry, just as that which occurred in the United States of Tocqueville's era. This, in turn, will eventually help to create a stable democratic polity in which the majority of the Brazilian population (that is, the poor) will truly participate for the first time.

This is not to say, however, that the road to change through the revindicações is not trodden without some difficulty. To be sure, as the São Paulo sample reveals, a number of problems have plagued the more activist lower-class CEBs over the years. Some of these originate from within the secular milieu, whereas others are directly traceable to the institutional Church.

Concerning the first category, one important problem that the Type VI

CEBs have faced over the years is a lack of popular acceptance. As many group leaders will confide, it has often been difficult to convince neighborhood residents that it was actually the local CEB that fought so hard for and won soon-taken-for-granted improvements such as running water and garbage pickup. "Even when things are accomplished by the CEB," one leader complained, "they still want to believe that it was the authorities who came in here and did it." Ironically, leaders also reported that many local residents became angry when they learned of the local CEBs' battles for infrastructural improvements. This was because, as property owners, they were required to pay partial installation costs and increased taxes for such things as sewers and water mains. This incredulity and, sometimes, anger on the part of local residents has tended to demoralize CEB members. It has also often denied the revindicações the broader basis of public support needed to continue and amplify their effects.

A second difficulty affecting the power of the revindicações has also originated from the community, but this time from the elite, as opposed to the grass-roots, level. Basically, the problem has had two dimensions. On the one hand, bribes offered by government officials, or even the rumors of bribes, have tended to create suspicion among group members and deaden enthusiasm about political action. On the other hand, electioneering has been a serious problem in at least some CEBs. In one case, vote-getting tactics, in the form of unrequested streetlight and running-water installation, preempted the CEB's own attempts to launch a campaign for these improvements. As the bishop of Lapa region, Dom Alfredo Novak, has suggested, government-sponsored urban renewal, even when it is undertaken out of genuine concern for the poor, is a major threat to the survival of the CEBs. Although the ends of the revindicações are most definitely achieved, CEB members are deprived of the citizenship-enhancing benefits of the process itself.[19] Even the hope inspired by campaign promises has posed a serious threat. In the wake of politicians' promises, it would seem, the revindicações lose their attractiveness as a means of effecting change.

The other difficulties that the Type VI groups in the São Paulo sample have faced are all Church-related, or internal to the CEBs. The first of these stems from the role of the pastoral agents, who often aid in CEB promotion and activation. Though the Church in São Paulo has seen the intervention of these individuals as indispensable to group life, their presence has also been quite disruptive to popular initiative. In many groups, for example, representatives of the Church have attempted to block "inappropriate" discussion (about birth control or abortion, for instance) or to screen anti-

Catholic influences. In one or two cases, the object of the pastoral agent's concern was the Brazilian Communist Party, which was reportedly seeking to draw CEB members from the Church. In others, concern was expressed about the potential influence of intra-institutional conservative forces such as Charismatic Renewal and the Society for the Preservation of Tradition, Family, and Property (TFP). Yet many CEB members expressed disdain for the rather undemocratic way in which pastoral agents sought to "protect" group participants from these elements. One person stated, "The Church gives space to the people, but only to a certain extent. But the Church should let ideas and influences enter the group, and then let the people decide if they want to act upon them or not." Another used the following analogy to express the same point. "The Church picks the person off the ground and puts him on a horse. The horse and rider begin to take off, but as soon as the horse starts to gather speed, the Church pulls back on the reins." As a result of such restriction, many leaders claimed, CEB members wishing to pursue social and political interests have become alienated, and other potential participants have been dissuaded from joining in the first place.[20]

The second Church-related difficulty arises from the more conservative CEB members' rejection of the more political aspects of the "option for the poor." As was noted in chapters 3 and 4, group members often disagree about participation in more politically explicit activities. This was especially true in the case of the revindicações. In both 1984 and 1988, up to half of group participants were avoiding involvement in this key activity. The strong presence of this religiously conservative element within the CEBs has certainly prevented the full realization of the groups' empowerment potential. Moreover, it has created within the CEBs a less-than-favorable climate for the eventual adoption of social causes more fundamental than the rather limited ones in which they have been involved.

Finally, the third Church-related problem affecting political activation concerns the CEBs' traditional overreliance on leadership—as invested primarily in the conselho. In most groups, in fact, the very success or failure of the revindicações has, to a considerable extent, depended on the skills and determination possessed by this core element. It is the conselho, for the most part, that discusses what problems should be tackled, the wording and preparation of petitions, how meetings should be arranged, and so forth. Such reliance carries with it at least some potential dangers where the neighborhood improvement strategy is concerned. First of all, reliance on an elite has made the process more vulnerable. It is anyone's guess as to how long the revindicações would have been undertaken in most groups in the absence of a few key players. Then, too, there has been a certain danger that as a result of elite control, the objectives of the revindicações might be subverted. Rather than helping to promote democratic participation and constructive cooperation, group leaders might be turning the process to their own advantage. According to at least one pastoral agent in 1984, this had already, in fact, occurred. The CEBs in his area, he claimed, were becoming a kind of "American dream machine" and were being manipulated by a small minority of CEB insiders to improve their own social status and material well-being. This warning was reiterated by Dom Luciano Mendes de Almeida, then bishop of Belém region and later president of the CNBB, who stated that "premature leadership and the effective use of power" have represented serious threats to the CEBs. Some leaders, he claimed, "have power which [they] use for non-evangelical purposes, directing it instead toward self-promotion and competitiveness."[21]

Conclusion

On the basis of the findings from the São Paulo sample in 1984 and 1988, it can be argued that the CEBs—specifically, the more politically active of the lower-class groups—can and do contribute directly to social change. They do this by helping to alter the way in which the poor think and feel about their role in Brazilian society. Through active engagement in the revindicações, the poor are taking up their rightful position as citizens with privileges and a duty to act collectively and honestly in the interests of their own and others' welfare.

In working toward this change, the CEBs have, not unexpectedly, run into certain difficulties originating in both society and the Church. Nevertheless, to this point, at least, they have pressed on, providing a shining example of just how the "option for the poor" can be implemented by and for its intended beneficiaries.

8
Changes
in Direction
-

In their ability to effect change within Brazilian society, the CEBs are in many ways only at the beginning of a potentially long journey. Though the groups do appear to have scored certain gains in citizenship building, there is still much work to be done. Indeed, as a collectivity, the CEBs touch only a very small portion of the Brazilian population. Clearly, they will have to widen their net considerably if the benefits they offer are to be extended to all those in need. Such a move is, in fact, crucial if the CEBs are to truly participate in the consolidation of democracy in Brazil, a process begun in the wake of the military's 1985 official transfer of power to civilians.

Yet even at this tentative stage in their development and growth, there is much evidence that the presence and role of the groups may be diminishing, perhaps irreversibly. An aide to Dom Fernando Penteado, the bishop responsible for the CEBs throughout the Southeast II region of the CNBB, lamented in a 1988 interview, "There is much movement, many projects ongoing at the level of the sector and the region. It is very impressive. But at the level of the CEBs, [participation] is very weak."[1]

The emergent signs of weakness in CEB activation are also apparent in the São Paulo sample. Here, there are some strong indications that the CEBs, especially the more advanced groups of the lower classes—which, it has been argued, are critical to the process of change—may be losing their effectiveness as agents of real social and political transformation.

Recent developments in CEB activation
Among the more politically mature, Type VI CEBs in the sample, a number of advances in political activation and certain concrete successes had most certainly been scored between 1984 and 1988. To begin with, it is

Table 7. Politically Related Beliefs and Attitudes of
Lower-Class (Type VI) CEB Members, 1984 and 1988 (in Percentages)

Belief or attitude	1984 (n=106)	1988 (n=69)
Describe Jesus Christ as "liberator"	39	77
Consciousness of social and political problems greater	58	67
Group membership offers opportunity to resolve problems	60	88

important to note that none of the groups of this type had disbanded by 1988. In fact, their number had increased from six to eight, representing just under half of the entire sample. In addition, the quality of the projects entertained and carried out during the previous four years did not appear to have varied from that originally witnessed. Five groups were involved in lobbying to obtain street paving, five mounted campaigns against poor bus service, four attempted to obtain health-care centers for their communities, and three lobbied for additional schools. Individually, groups also lobbied for and obtained, in most cases, better police protection, leisure areas, walkways, water, sewers, streetlights, public telephones, traffic lights, and legal land title for residents.

By 1988, it was also apparent that intragroup heterogeneity and conflict, shown in chapter 7 to be factors frequently hampering Type VI CEB effectiveness in the political sphere, were diminishing. As can be observed from Table 7, members' attitudes had become much more uniform in a number of key respects. First, respondents were much more likely in 1988 than in 1984 to describe Jesus Christ as a "liberator," in accordance with the teaching of more progressive elements within the Brazilian Catholic Church. Moreover, as was already noted in chapter 7, CEB members were more likely to claim enhanced political consciousness as a result of their CEB experience, and much more prone to indicate that their group had offered them a chance to confront the social and political difficulties that they saw facing Brazil and the Church. A similar trend toward homogeneity and harmony can be observed in members' politically related behavior (Table 8). To begin with, there exists a striking change in the degree of member participation in group leadership. Whereas only 48 percent of group members sat on leadership councils in 1984, this number increased to 68 percent in 1988. Increases, albeit slight, are also apparent

Table 8. Politically Related Actions and Behavior of
Lower-Class (Type VI) CEB Members, 1984 and 1988 (in Percentages)

Action or behavior	1984 (n=106)	1988 (n=69)
Participation in one or more civil associations within 5 years	40	43
Participate in group leadership	48	68
Participate in consciousness raising	60	61
Participate in revindicações	*	59

*Figure not available from 1984 data.

in members' engagement in political consciousness raising, and in their extra-CEB participation in civil associations or functions. The same appears to be true of members' participation in the revindicações, although comparative numbers for 1984 are not available. At that time, however, qualitative research in the groups in question suggested that participation rates were at or under about 50 percent.

Nevertheless, although these findings may lend optimism to those who would see the more advanced lower-class CEBs as continuing to play a strong and vital role in the process of societal transformation, further investigation reveals a less-than-encouraging portrait of CEB activation. For one thing, the Type VI groups have diminished in size. In 1984, the six CEBS involved in the revindicações claimed, on average, a membership of 36. By 1988, the eight CEBs so engaged possessed only 23 members on average. Moreover, considerable member turnover is in evidence. Though the groups had actually become smaller, over 40 percent of their participants joined after 1984.

Upon reexamining Table 5 (see chapter 5), it also becomes apparent that among the Type VI and lower-class groups generally, there has occurred something of a move toward the more devotional side of Catholic practice. As the table shows, attention to more traditional functions has increased somewhat more dramatically since 1984 than that given to innovative functions. It would appear that with the choice between initiating Bible study/charity circles or reflection/political-discussion groups, the former has won out.

This renewed emphasis on the devotional is clearly seen in alterations that group members in the more advanced lower-class CEBs have made to their community centers. Between 1984 and 1988, members spent considerable time, energy, and money in improving these. In virtually all groups, party and Sunday-school rooms had been completed, walls painted, curtains purchased, and sound systems acquired. In short, given these improvements and the growing tendency toward the offering of more traditional activities, the local CEB community center is becoming more and more like the local parish church.

Perhaps the most serious change that the Type VI CEBs have undergone concerns the way in which the revindicações have come to be undertaken in most groups. Despite an increase in the number of groups claiming to offer this activity, and a rise in the number of participants ostensibly involved, the quality and the quantity of community-project activity have eroded somewhat over the years. To be sure, in 1988, all of the Type VI CEBs still formally supported the concept of the revindicações. Yet, at the time of the research, only one of the groups was actually involved in activity of this kind. Of the remaining seven, three no longer undertook the community projects as a group per se. Instead, group members participated, on behalf of the CEB, in revindicações organized at higher institutional levels. The other four had suspended participation in the revindicações altogether. In the words of their leaders, these groups were *meio-parado* (more or less stopped) where the revindicações were concerned, and would likely remain so until the "necessity" for further action arose. Significantly, this attitude toward the projects stands in sharp contrast to that in 1984, when the revindicações were almost universally considered more important as ends in themselves than as means. It is also important to note that even if the revindicações were considered simply a means, there was certainly no lack of "necessary" work still to be accomplished in 1988 in most neighborhoods.

Factors contributing to diminished CEB activity

This trend to the externalization of political function, or outright dormancy, in the most advanced lower-class CEBs can be explained in a number of ways. In some respects, it might be seen simply as the outcome of a power struggle between the more conservative and more progressive CEB factions first witnessed in 1984. True enough, by 1988, conflict did appear to have abated, and greater consensus was evident where political action was concerned. This does not mean, however, that the more conservative CEB participants had become any more willing to take action. Rather than battling it out, they may simply have struck a certain accommodation with the progressives in the CEBs in a truly Brazilian fashion—namely, that of compromise. In effect, the conservatives may have agreed to accept the language of political action while, in fact, enhancing devotional practices. The progressives, for their part, may have received support for their political beliefs but agreed to participate politically outside their group.

Second, there are also the pacifying consequences of bureaucratization to consider in any assessment of the CEBs' changing status. In keeping with authors such as Weber and Robert Michels, it might be argued that as the groups have become more institutionalized, their leadership has mellowed and the passion for revolutionary activity has waned.[2] Collective goals have remained, but increasing attention has been paid to institutional and housekeeping matters. Hence appears the seeming anomaly in the more advanced groups of upholding the necessity and purpose of the revindicações while at the same time striving to create a miniparish or church out of the local community center.

A third important factor impeding CEB activity is related to the prevailing political climate in Brazil after 1985. On the one hand, the removal of the military and the advent of civilian democracy has eliminated part of the CEBs' raison d'être. As an aide to Bishop Penteado explained, "During the dictatorship, the groups had an enemy to confront. It gave them strength. But now, in democracy, they have weakened. Their seige mentality has weakened."[3] On the other hand, owing to the grave political inertia exhibited by the country's newly elected civilian politicians, there existed in São Paulo and all of Brazil by 1988 a great sense of disillusionment with the political process. "After the elections," a CEB leader revealed, "the people were very happy. They had a lot of hope. But the politicians did nothing, and the people were let down." "More and more," added another, "they [CEB members] find it's just not worth it to complain."

The fourth and final factor accounting for the turn in CEB fortune— perhaps the most critical factor of all—is Church influence. As I argued in the Introduction, the Brazilian Catholic Church had, since at least 1960, been a strong supporter of CEB growth and activation. In more recent years, however, it has become increasingly confused in the way it views the phenomenon.

Recent changes in Brazilian Catholicism

This seeming turnaround on the part of the Church coincides with a much broader transformation in Brazilian Catholicism that can be traced to the early 1980s.[4] Not only has the upper hierarchy become more fractious, a tendency toward conservatism has become increasingly apparent.

The Church as an institution has also returned to previous modes of political influence, and appears to be abandoning its support for grass-roots movements, in favor of direct pressure on political policymakers.

On the surface, admittedly, the Brazilian Church's commitment to the content and implementation of its "option for the poor" would appear to be holding firm.[5] Within the structure of the progressive CNBB, for example, little seems to have changed since the late 1970s and early 1980s— since the days of intense military-religious conflict. In April 1987, the presidency of the CNBB was passed uneventfully to Dom Luciano Mendes de Almeida, who immediately issued several documents in support of those suffering under the weight of political and economic injustice in Brazil. One such statement warned of an impending social convulsion resulting from the government's persistent inability to stabilize Brazil's "roller-coaster" economy. In another release, Dom Luciano decried the "frightening misery" pervading the Brazilian population—misery, he argued, promoted by a government policy "that maintains [in Brazil] the lowest salaries in the world."

A number of statements and actions of individual bishops have also upheld the impression that all is well with the "option for the poor." During 1987, Dom Angélico Sândalo Bernardino, auxiliary bishop to Cardinal Arns of São Paulo and longtime activist, stepped up his involvement with the issue of squatters' rights in the poor districts of his region. Accusing government authorities of "practicing the greatest act of civil disobedience and anarchy in the country" for denying the poor access to decent housing, Dom Angélico called for those involved to resist expulsion and, if necessary, forcibly occupy the São Paulo state housing secretariat. Similarly, before his election as CNBB head, Dom Luciano Mendes de Almeida publicly advocated the use of civil disobedience as "an instrument the poorest [segment of the] population must use, should economic measures adopted by the government come to be prejudicial to them."

The continued strength and vibrancy of the "option for the poor" is ostensibly demonstrated, as well, in the work undertaken by various Church groups and individuals directly involved with human-rights issues —work that has continued, for the most part, unabated. The Church's Pastoral Land Commission—despite occasional accusations of misuse of funds and inciting to violence—still, as in the past, offers legal protection and moral support to peasants victimized by the actions of unscrupulous landholders. The work of the Native Missionary Council (CIMI), for its part, has even taken on added significance, given the threat to native people from the destruction of the rain forests.

Outwardly, then, all seems to be in order with the "option." Dom Helder Câmara, in fact, one of the original architects and supporters of the Church's social-justice current, claimed to be extremely pleased with the Church's state of political activation in the latter half of the 1980s. The Church's position, he stated, was a sign that it was continuing to assume its responsibility to "confront the situation."

However, with respect to both content and implementation, a number of anomalies have appeared in the Church's commitment to social justice. To begin with, a growing and unprecedented amount of dissidence regarding the Church's political orientation has been emerging from within the ranks of the episcopate. Whereas some bishops have stalwartly upheld the cause of social justice, others have worked very hard to deny it. In 1987, for example, Archbishop Eugenio Sales of Rio de Janeiro unsuccessfully attempted to scuttle a planned encounter of black sisters, seminary students, and priests from 10 states who sought to discuss race, political participation, and Catholicism. Sales justified this move by arguing that the conference would almost certainly do further injury to what he felt was an already fragile "ecclesiastical unity" in Brazil. In that same year, the archbishop of Maceió disbanded the local "political-education" team of the northeast region's long-standing Basic Education Movement (MEB) because of its connections with the radical left, especially the Communist Party of Brazil. In the words of the archbishop, the action was taken "to preserve the authority of the Pope and to ensure that the pastoral mission of the Church would not be depreciated." Two years later, José Cardoso Sobrinho, archbishop of Recife, undertook similar action, purging four members of the local Pastoral Land Commission for their involvement with working-class political movements.

Among the Brazilian episcopate, there has also emerged a renewed preoccupation with more traditional religious matters, which, contrary to the dictates of the "option for the poor," is often expressed at the expense of certain sectors of the poor and oppressed. In January 1987, Belo Horizonte archbishop Dom Serafim Araújo lambasted the Minas Gerais state government for promoting the use of condoms to prevent AIDS. This, he said, would serve to institutionalize homosexuality. Similarly, Dom Benedito Vieira, archbishop of Uberaba, issued a stern warning to federal government authorities reportedly working on a family-planning program for Brazil. Though claiming to recognize the need for family planning, he stated that it must be undertaken only "under moral [natural] conditions." And finally, in an attempt to preserve doctrinal purity, Bishop Clóvis Rodrigues angered the Brazilian Foreign Ministry when he nearly scuttled a visit by the South African Anglican bishop Desmond Tutu. Rodrigues had telephoned Tutu at home to inform him that an ecumenical ceremony planned during his visit would involve *candomblé* (a traditional form of Afro-Brazilian worship) and that it would not, therefore, be appropriate for him (Rodrigues) to attend.

One thing that must be made clear is that this tendency to more conservative views and actions is by no means restricted to those Church leaders who might, in any case, be deemed traditionalists. Even many of those formerly most vocal in defense of the social-justice theme have apparently moved toward the political center. In the spring of 1986, for instance, Cardinal Arns of São Paulo called in the local military police, a body he had formerly fought tooth and nail, to disperse angry students at the Pontifícia Universidade Católica (of which he is chancellor). The students had begun to riot after being prohibited from viewing Godard's controversial film on the life of the Virgin Mary, *Je vous salue Marie*. It was rumored, as well, that a subsequent presidential ban on the film in Brazil was instigated primarily at Dom Paulo's request. Furthermore, Dom Luciano Mendes de Almeida, in his capacity as president of the CNBB, publicly scolded Leonardo Boff, famed liberation theologist and champion of the oppressed, for remarks he had made on returning from a trip to the USSR. To Boff's claim that there existed no restrictions to liberty in the Soviet Union, Dom Luciano retorted that it was difficult to "understand [the theologian's remarks] given the conditions imposed upon dissidents [in that country]."

Perhaps the most telling sign of the shift in episcopal thinking about the "option for the poor" is the way in which the bishops have begun to deal with government authorities. In the years following the coup of 1964, as an expression of its solidarity with the cause of the poor, the institutional Church had broken off its formal ties with the State. It appears that after 1985, however, the Church moved once again toward more direct involvement in the affairs of government.

Since the election of José Sarney as the first civilian president of Brazil in over 20 years, the Church, in fact, has been a constant fixture in the halls of power. Dom Luciano Mendes de Almeida, for example, as secretary-general of the CNBB, had been a frequent visitor to the presidential palace and, at one time, was thought to be one of Sarney's closest confidants. In his capacity as president of the bishops' conference, furthermore, he has certainly been less than shy about calling on influential power brokers to resolve Church problems. In late August 1987, he met with several congressmen to demand a parliamentary inquiry into "fraudulent" press criticism of the CNBB's Indigenous Missionary Council (CIMI). Even as late as May 1989, he requested that the president personally intervene on behalf of agricultural workers engaged in disputes with landowners in Rio Grande do Sul and Bahia states.

At a more general level of interaction, other Church leaders have consulted with government officials on a number of specific issues since late 1985. In early 1987, for instance, a Church delegation met with several ministers to discuss plans for the military and economic occupation of the 6,500-kilometer-long Amazon frontier. Still other talks have focused on measures necessary to ensure the safety of Catholic missionaries working among native people in remote parts of the country.

There has also been strong evidence of increased Church involvement in electoral politics and political decision making—involvement highly reminiscent of Church action during the 1930s, when Church leaders attempted to influence public policy-making through such things as voting "leagues" and high-level influence peddling. Before the 1986 general elections, some of the bishops, including outspoken progressives such as São Paulo's Cardinal Arns and Bauru's Cândido Padim, released detailed lists of candidates deemed worthy of Church support. Such activity was unheard of during elections held just four years earlier, when Church leaders took great pains to educate voters politically without appearing to favor any one political party. Furthermore, again in a manner resembling that of earlier days, the Church planned and executed an intense lobbying campaign (through its various pastoral commissions) to influence legislators engaged in writing the country's new constitution. This move was officially announced in January 1987 by Dom Luciano Mendes de Almeida, then secretary-general of the CNBB, who argued that the action was necessary to ensure that "ethical values" were included in the assembly's final document. The four areas specifically targeted for inclusion in the constitution by the CNBB, moreover, are interesting in both content and order of priority. Indicative of a move away from the "option for the poor," the first priority was to be the preservation of the traditional family (through the prohibition of divorce), and the last, the "right to life" issue, with agrarian reform and the rights of labor sandwiched in the middle.

Why did the Church begin to move in these directions? A number of explanations may be offered. The one most obvious influence originates within the Church in Rome, which has increasingly attempted to bring more activist national Churches, such as Brazil's, under stricter Vatican control—part of what many have referred to as a process of Romanization. In part, at least, there can be little question that in downplaying the social-justice theme, some members of the episcopate in Brazil have simply capitulated to pressure exerted by the pope and other leading Church figures to curtail their overt involvement in certain political causes, and to bring Brazilian Church policy, generally, into line with that of the Vatican.

Vatican interference with the "option for the poor" began as early as 1984, when, to assess the intrusion of liberationist principles, Rome instigated a review of seminary instruction in more progressive Brazilian archdioceses. In Cardinal Arns's São Paulo, this review was undertaken by Cardinal Josef Hoeffner of the Vatican's Sacred Congregation for Catholic Education. Though all seemed in order, Hoeffner nevertheless issued stern warnings to archdiocesan personnel that in no sense should the liberationist image of Christ as "revolutionary figure" be invoked in undertaking action to assist the poor. Around this time, as well, the Vatican began to show a preference for the appointment of more moderate clerics to key diocesan posts in Brazil. In May 1984, for example, the Church named José Freire Falcão—a well-known opponent of more radical forms of liberation theology—as archbishop of the capital, Brasília. Concurrent with this appointment, rumors began to surface that even the outspoken Cardinal Arns of São Paulo would be removed to a "safer" posting, perhaps even outside Brazil.

In 1985, Church leaders turned their sights on leading liberation theologians such as Leonardo and Clodovis Boff. The former was censured during that year by Rome's Sacred Congregation for the Doctrine of the Faith for "errors and deviations" committed in a book he had written entitled *Igreja: Carisma e poder* (1981; Church: Charisma and power). Accused of having drawn too closely on secular Marxism in his writings on Church and society, Boff was prohibited from writing and speaking publicly for eighteen months. The Vatican later rescinded the banning order, but only after the news of its imposition had reached the four corners of the Catholic world. Clodovis Boff, another important liberationist, also ran into difficulty both at home and abroad. In Rome, he had been forbidden to teach in a school run by his own order (Servitas), and in Brazil, was barred by Cardinal Eugenio Sales of Rio de Janeiro from instructing in all schools within his jurisdiction.

As if to drive home the Vatican's concerns over the orientation of the Brazilian Church, Pope John Paul II, after 1985, convoked an unprecedented series of special meetings with various groups of bishops from throughout Brazil. By March 1986, nearly 200 Brazilian bishops had visited Rome.[6] The most significant of these encounters was held in early 1986, and brought together all 21 of the country's leading Church officials. Ostensibly, the pope had wanted to smooth over the hard feelings among the bishops that resulted from Leonardo Boff's harsh treatment at the hands of the Congregation of the Faith. In the final analysis, however, the meetings appear to have been directed primarily toward illustrating the limits of Vatican tolerance for Brazilian Church involvement in overt political causes at the expense of concern for more traditional religious matters. This message was reiterated in 1988, when the Vatican turned its attention once again to Brazil's more outspoken Churchmen. Dom Pedro Casaldáliga, bishop of São Felix do Araguaia and virulent defender of liberation theology, was subjected to restrictions on writing and travel similar to those imposed on Leonardo Boff three years earlier. CNBB president Luciano Mendes de Almeida, formerly the auxiliary bishop of São Paulo, was removed to a conservative diocese in the interior of Minas Gerais state. In a seemingly related move, Rome also threatened to split the domain of Cardinal Arns into separate dioceses, thus removing his seat of power.

In 1989, the Vatican continued its assault. In the spring of that year, it made good on previous threats to dismantle Brazil's largest archdiocese, creating four new ecclesiastical units and reducing São Paulo to its basic core. During the same year, conservatives Lucas Neves and José Cardoso Sobrinho were appointed as heads of the Salvador and Recife archdioceses, respectively. Finally, Leonardo Boff was silenced once again for his wayward views, and in a very dramatic move, the Vatican's Congregation for Catholic Education closed two seminaries in Brazil known for their promotion of liberation theology. Both of these were situated in northeastern Brazil and had been established by the respected Church activist Dom Helder Câmara, former archbishop of Recife.

Other factors contributing to alterations in the "option for the poor"—factors that have also affected the CEBs directly, to some extent—are external to the Church and originate in Brazil's present political transition. Considering the history of the Church's adversarial relationship with military governments since 1964, and the contribution of this relationship to the definition and implementation of the "option for the poor," there can, in fact, be little question that Brazil's recent redemocratization has had a profound effect on the bishops' thinking.

First, with much of the machinery of repression removed, it can be argued that the bishops, quite simply, no longer have anything concrete to react against—no reactionary, dictatorial, monolithic evil to tackle. As a result, the unity of the Church has eroded somewhat, and the necessity of undertaking immediate social or political action has lessened. Second, Brazil's nascent democratic government, while ostensibly more palatable politically to the Church, has caused new concerns for the hierarchy in an old area—morality. Whereas Brazil's former military leaders considered themselves moral purists, with democracy has come a tendency for political leaders to cater to liberalized tastes and desires, which are often in conflict with official Church teaching. In response to this rather unanticipated eventuality, it may well be argued, the bishops have been forced to divert their attention away from more politically charged matters.

Consequences of Church change for the CEBs

Such dramatic changes in statements and policy related to the "option" have been very much reflected in the way the CEBs and their role have come to be conceptualized by the upper hierarchy. After 1988, for example, references to the CEBs as such in official documents became almost non-existent. In the CNBB's most recent planning document, *Diretrizes gerais da Ação pastoral da Igreja no Brasil, 1987–1990*, as well as in *Igreja: Comunhão e missão na evangelização dos povos* (1988), the term CEB is rarely used. What frequently appears in its place is the generic *comunidade eclesial,* which refers not only to CEBs but to dioceses, parishes, families, and Church-related associations and movements. Nor are the CEBs singled out as an item for special concern among pastoral priorities, as they were in previous documents. In regional documents, as well, such as the archdiocese of São Paulo's *5° plano de pastoral, 1987–1990* (1987), the CEBs were dropped altogether as a priority.

Officially, at least, this lack of emphasis in Church documents has not been due to neglect. Rather, as Dom Fernando Penteado pointed out in a recent interview, special attention is no longer necessary because the CEBs and CEB activation are proceeding very well and no longer require direct assistance from the upper hierarchy.[7]

It is difficult to see, however, how this could be so. To begin with, when examined in context, growth rates for the CEBs have been less dramatic than would appear at first glance. As was seen in chapter 2, the number of CEBs officially recorded in the archdiocese of São Paulo, for instance, increased from 765 to 875 between 1983 and 1988. This increase of 14 percent roughly corresponds to the population growth of the archdiocese over the same period (from about 11 million to about 13 million). Furthermore, despite an easing in political restrictions under the new civilian administration, the economy has worsened over the years. Between September 1987 and May 1988, inflation consistently ran between 15 percent and 20 percent per month, and earnings decreased in real terms by approximately 30 percent. Moreover, economic growth and unemployment rates have moved up and down more dramatically from month to month than they would from year to year in developed countries. The continuing crisis would thus seem to call for greater, not weaker, Church support for CEB activation.

The official mission of the CEBs, to the extent that one exists, has now, it appears, come to be tied to their potential for building leadership. The new vision of the CEBs that emerges from Church documents is that the groups are merely one of many means of effecting social action. In essence, the CEBs and other similar types of lay groups and associations are no longer viewed as agents acting autonomously in the name of the Church. Rather, they are to provide militants to operate within existing secular bodies such as labor unions and popular movements. As one 1988 CNBB document stated, the hope of the Church is that the CEBs and other groups, "with their strictly ecclesial function [, will] develop human qualities which serve to mold real Christian militants [who] will become real 'planters' of a new political structure in the country." [8]

This growing lack of emphasis on the CEBs and CEB activation has taken a direct toll on the success of the CEBs in various parts of Brazil, as authors such as Della Cava and Doimo have noted.[9] In the case of the more advanced, lower-class groups in the São Paulo sample, this is especially true. In effect, there has been a severe shortage of both the moral and the material support required to keep the CEBs involved in the quest for the "new society."

For leaders of those CEBs most heavily involved in the revindicações, already dejected by the failure of elected governments to respond to popular concerns, the Church's actions in this regard were a severe blow to morale. In 1988, CEB organizers and activists spoke openly of "abandonment" by the hierarchy and the "death" of the "Church of the poor." Explained one CEB leader, "The Church no longer gives encouragement to those lay people who really want to engage in political action," adding, with a note of sadness, "the Church which you [the researcher] knew in 1984 exists no longer." One direct consequence, this leader suggested, is that CEB members "have left to fight in the unions and political parties," unable to "accept the situation within the Church any longer." Needless to say, this view clashes with the Church's vision of CEB-member participation in civil associations and movements as part of the groups' official mandate.

Concrete evidence of a weakening in institutional support for CEB activities is, similarly, not difficult to find. In the Type VI CEBs, it is apparent that inactivation where the revindicações are concerned has been due in no small measure to an absence of leadership and guidance from the local Church. After about 1987, intentionally or due to neglect, priests, nuns, and other pastoral agents were no longer being made available in sufficient quantity or quality to assist the CEBs in their efforts to undertake the revindicações. By 1988, none of the eight groups claiming to be involved in the revindicações were accompanied by pastoral agents. In most cases, pastoral agents had been pulled or had voluntarily removed themselves and were never replaced. Five of the groups, it is true, were visited regularly by local nuns or, in one or two cases, by seminarians. But these individuals, often involved in several groups, were said by group leaders to maintain a low-key presence, and did not form part of the groups' conselhos, as had occurred in 1984.

Comments of CEB leaders attested to their dismay over this lack of concrete support. Stated one leader, "When the Oblates left, the people became disheartened. . . . This [the new parish] priest, he does everything correctly, but he gives us no support in our work. He doesn't stop us, but he doesn't help us." Another CEB leader similarly explained the lack of revindicações in her group by referring to the current vacuum of institutional support. "The [new] priest helps nothing. He talks about politics, but when we arrive [at the parish house] to consult him, he heads out the back door."

Conclusion

After 1984, the more advanced, lower-class CEBs in the São Paulo sample appeared to be well on the road to making a genuine contribution to social and political change in Brazil. Not only did they transform the face of their neighborhoods, it was also evident that through their victories at the community level, participants in the more advanced CEBs were at least beginning to gain an understanding of the political process and of their contribution as citizens to the building of a stable, democratic Brazil.

With the sample CEBs' key community-action function inhibited by a variety of secular and Church-related factors, this process of citizenship building is slowing to a crawl. Rather than pursuing visions of the new society, in fact, the CEBs seem to be embarking on a new path. They now appear to be more concerned with establishing their status as bona fide miniparishes than with retaining their status as nuclei of popular dissent, resistance, and political education.

Conclusion

This study began as an exercise in understanding the essential nature and thrust of the Brazilian CEB phenomenon—what the CEBs are and what they do. To this point, a good deal of territory has been covered as I have examined data from CEBs in the archdiocese of São Paulo, as well as other relevant social-scientific research.

Yet, for those who would seek a definitive characterization of the Brazilian CEBs, much would appear to be lacking. If there is one single aspect of the CEBs that this study has emphasized, it is the tremendous diversity of form and action that marks the groups. To deny this heterogeneity, or to restrict the definition of the CEBs to one particular form, is to deny the very essence of the phenomenon.

What the CEBs are, at the most elementary level, are communities of lay Catholics who share a common social situation and a common commitment to the "option for the poor." Still and all, however, they take on a variety of shapes and organizational characteristics, and manage to attract individuals from virtually all walks of life—young and old, rich and poor, male and female.

What the CEBs do, in the most basic sense, is to implement a religiously rooted commitment to this-worldly justice. Yet, here again, the way in which they do this varies considerably. Some CEBs may focus on more devotional activities, others on social or political consciousness raising, and still others on more concrete issues such as land reform and infrastructural improvement.

Moreover, whereas they all have implications for Brazilian society, they are differentially involved in the process of social change. Some of the more elementary groups may be seen as contributing comparatively little in this regard. Nevertheless, they still serve to awaken the laity generally to Brazilian problems and the necessity of finding solutions. Among the CEBs of the middle classes, especially, this is an important process, given the historical role that the middle classes have played in facilitating or, at very least, allowing revolutionary activity to occur. As authors from Weber to Barrington Moore have pointed out, social and political change of a type envisioned by the Church rarely takes place without the approval or active participation of intermediary social strata favorably disposed to such change.[i]

Among the more advanced CEBs of the poor, a much more direct influence on social change may be observed. As they engage in political discussion and undertake concrete struggles to improve the local quality of life, the lower classes are learning the fundamentals of good citizenship. Out of this can come changes in the status quo of class relations in Brazil, and a more just social order.

Amid this diversity, there is, however, at least one constant in the life of the CEBs—the relationship the groups maintain with the Brazilian Church. Despite the assertions and, indeed, hopes of many with respect to CEB autonomy, the CEBs remain tied to the agenda of the hierarchy in a variety of ways. Firmly rooted in the traditional parish structure of Catholicism, they are monitored by pastoral agents and subject to penalty for straying too far from Church teaching.

Such linkages have been extremely important in the activation and development of a mature CEB phenomenon in Brazil. As one priest working in a lower-class district in eastern São Paulo commented, "The Church is the engine which pulls the cars," that is, the CEBs.

Significantly, though, these ties have also, very recently, proven equally conducive to a partial dismantling of much of what the CEBs have accomplished to this point. In São Paulo, especially, a diminished emphasis on the CEBs at all institutional levels has directly contributed to a certain paralyzation of the CEBs' key community-action function and, thus, of the process of citizenship building. As at least a few other authors have noted, this appears to be occurring in other parts of Brazil as well.

This is not to say that the CEBs' future course is now irreversibly set. Indeed, in the short run, at least, the Church is not about to cut the groups adrift. Abandoning the CEBs would deal a severe blow to the Church's self-image as defender of the oppressed. Moreover, the fragility of the current social, political, and economic situations in Brazil demands that Church leaders, as a moral duty, uphold their defense of the weakest sectors of the population.

Neither are the CEBs already dead. For the moment, at least, this is far from the truth. In most parts of Brazil, the phenomenon continues to thrive, albeit in somewhat modified form, with many groups still engaged in a host of devotional and political activities.

In terms of what the groups represent symbolically, as well, the CEBs are still very much alive. By their very existence, the groups continue to inspire the faithful at all levels of the Church to stay involved in the effort to create new opportunities for intra- and extra-Church activation. Such is the case not only in Brazil, but in many other parts of the world where the Brazilian CEBs have achieved a kind of folk status. Aside from the tens of thousands of base communities in Latin America, CEBs are now known to have spread to the Philippines, Africa, and even many countries of the developed world. In Italy and Holland, several hundred have been counted. In Canada and the United States, among the urban poor, refugees, and even the middle classes, the CEB phenomenon is growing.[2] In all of these countries, the Brazilian base-community phenomenon serves as a beacon of hope and a model for emulation.

Yet, in the long run, if trends within the institutional Church continue, the demise of the Brazilian CEBs—in their present form, at least—and their example to Catholics everywhere is almost certain. Some authors, such as Adriance and Kevin Neuhouser, suggest that to some extent, the CEBs have built up their own momentum and may be able to resist any and all attempts by the hierarchy of the Church to suppress them.[3] If the findings of this study are correct with respect to institutional power over the CEBs, however, the groups are unlikely to survive in the face of increased hierarchical opposition or indifference. The same institution that has nurtured the CEBs seems well positioned to orchestrate their downfall, and capable of doing so, should this be its desire.

Regardless of its ultimate fate, however, the CEB phenomenon will likely remain, for some time, an object of intense focus among social scientists. Even in the CEBs' present state, there are certainly many aspects of group life that are beyond the scope of this study and that are still to be explored.

One fertile area for further investigation is the complexity of CEB relations with the institutional Church. Indeed, considering the very strong relationship between institutional transformation and CEB fate posited here, this would seem an imperative Another aspect of the groups deserving of attention is the relationship the groups have built with the scores of popular movements that have arisen in Brazil during the 1980s. To what extent, it might be asked, is the political effectiveness of the CEBs now being transferred to other areas of secular endeavor?

Further research might also be undertaken on the way in which group members relate to one another as members of religio-political communities. Similarly, investigation of the way in which CEB participants perceive and relate to both Church teaching and secular ideology would also seem in order.

Certainly, however, the principal question that will capture the attention of CEB analysts in the future—and with good reason—is how, specifically, and under what conditions the CEBs will continue to implement their mandate for social change. An answer to this question will require, if the findings of my study are correct, intense scrutiny of alterations in thinking and action at the level of the institutional Church—especially the upper hierarchy.

Also worth noting in the days ahead will be the CEBs' own attempts to come to grips with the overt and more subtle forms of institutional control that will largely determine their fate. Rather interestingly, there are now at least some indications that the CEBs may be attempting to distance themselves from the institution—in effect, taking their fate and future activation into their own hands. At the national CEB encounter held in Duque de Caxias, Rio de Janeiro state, in July 1989, group representatives and sympathizers openly discussed the necessity of utilizing more overt forms of political action in pursuit of social change. Some held that direct involvement in politics should be left to the political parties. Many, however, advocated the formation of a CEB-directed representative association. As the liberation theologian Clodovis Boff recounted, "The party-political issue emerged in an irreversible manner in the CEBs, because they understood that in order to transform society they needed to use the tool called party."[4]

The formation of such a representative body could mark a crucial pass for the CEBs. Certainly, it would pose a considerable threat to institutional control—a threat that would not be taken lightly by Church leaders in Brazil. Yet, given the increasingly negative orientation of the Church to enhanced CEB activation in the spheres of society and politics, and however unlikely its success, such a strategy may be the only option left to the CEBs if they are ever to realize their potential as tranformers of society.

Appendix

This study was based on field research conducted in the archdiocese of São Paulo, Brazil, from January to June 1984 and again during April and May 1988. Data were collected from written materials, from members of the local hierarchy, and from a number of CEBs chosen from various areas throughout the archdiocese. The following sections present detailed explanations of how the research area and CEB sample were chosen, as well as a description of the data-collection techniques employed. Translations of actual interview schedules and questionnaires are presented in a separate section at the end of this appendix.

The research area

The selection of a research frame within which to conduct the study was not an easy task, for the Brazilian CEBs tend to constitute a national, as opposed to a regional, phenomenon. Any number of areas could, in fact, have been chosen, but ultimately São Paulo was selected because, at the time of the research, it had certain specific characteristics that made it especially attractive for research of this type. First, the archdiocese was the largest in Brazil in terms of land area and population. Second, it was quite diverse with respect to land-use patterns and social characteristics. There were, for example, a number of well-defined districts, ranging from urban high-density to suburban low-density, that were inhabited by persons of widely varying class backgrounds. Third, São Paulo was considered to be one of the most politically progressive ecclesiastical units in Brazil, suggesting that large numbers of CEBs would be available for study.

The CEB sample

Once São Paulo had been selected as the principal area of investigation, a sample of CEBs were chosen for intense study. The objectives of the study called for an examination of as many groups as possible from as many different parts of the archdiocese as possible, with an eye to maintaining, for purposes of comparison, a rough balance between CEBs originating in different social and geographical settings. To this end, a stratified random-sampling plan was devised and executed in the following stages.

The first task was to narrow the research frame to make the sampling process more manageable. This job was relatively easy because the arch-diocese was already divided into nine separate episcopal regions (or quasi-dioceses) of roughly equal population, each with its own resident bishop and local system of governance. Using a government study (GESP, 1977) that divides the municipality of São Paulo into homogeneous areas ac-cording to the physical properties of districts and the class origins of their inhabitants, a rough socioeconomic profile of each region was developed. Then I selected three of the nine regions that best represented the essential characteristics of the archdiocese as a whole. The first of these, Região Sé, was chosen because it lies at the heart of the archdiocese and is strictly urban and predominantly middle-class (although pockets of urban slum-dwellers are also present). The two other regions, Santo Amaro and São Miguel, lie to the south and east of Sé, respectively, and were selected be-cause they are partly urban and affluent but also take in huge expanses of São Paulo's suburban periphery, where the poor predominate.

The next stage in the sampling process involved the selection of subre-gional units, or sectors, from the three regions. One more affluent and one less affluent sector were to be chosen from among the five or six extant, on average, within each region. To make this selection, each of the 20 or so subregional units had to be ranked using the homogeneous-area rank-ing scheme described earlier. Sectors were given scores ranging from 1 (urban high-density, upper-class) to 8 (suburban periphery, lower-class). One less affluent sector was then chosen at random from among those with the lowest scores in each region, and one more affluent sector from among those with the highest scores. For example, Sé region possesses six sectors in total; two of rank 1, two of rank 2, and two of rank 4. Using the statistical mean of these scores (2.3) as a break point, we chose one sector from among those with ranks above 2.3, and one from those with ranks lower than 2.3.

Once two somewhat opposite sectors had been selected from each of our three regions, sample parishes were then identified for intense study. To provide a fair cross section of these, it was decided that two would be picked at random from each sector (sectors contain, on average, about six parishes). To ensure, moreover, that these parishes generally conformed to the characterization of the subregional unit that was previously established, local pastors were immediately contacted by telephone and quizzed briefly about social conditions in their areas of jurisdiction. Once the physical and socioeconomic statuses of the parishes were confirmed, meetings were solicited with the pastors to personally request permission to conduct research in their areas.

The final task was to select individual CEBs for study. It was intended that 2 groups would be chosen at random from each of the 12 sample parishes. This, I felt, would provide a fairly large, yet manageable, sample, and also allow for comparisons between sister CEBs existing under nearly identical social and geographical circumstances. The selection of pairs of CEBs within parishes was contingent, however, on their availability for study; and in a few cases, unfortunately, no more than one CEB was operational.

The CEBs that were ultimately chosen for investigation were picked from lists of lay groups provided by the parish pastor. To be considered candidates for random selection, parish CEBs had to conform to the basic definition of the groups that the Church has adopted. Specifically, they had to be (1) communities, in the sense that they were composed of people who were neighbors and thus shared living conditions; (2) ecclesial, insofar as they were composed of people who considered themselves to be a part of the Roman Catholic Church; and (3) basic, in that they consisted of ordinary lay people. Naturally, assessments of CEB status relied heavily on the evaluation of the local priest, who determined whether the groups under consideration actually met these criteria. Once the selection process was completed, however, the presence of these basic attributes in the CEB was confirmed before proceeding.

A total of 22 CEBs were selected, following these procedures. Eleven were located in urban middle-class districts with a weighted average homogeneous-area rank of 3.9. The balance were situated in lower-class areas (average rank 7.2) either on the periphery of São Paulo ($n=9$) or in urban slums ($n=2$).

The precise location and basic statistics of each of the 22 sample CEBs, both at the initial point of investigation and for 1988, are summarized in Tables 9 and 10.

Table 9. Basic Characteristics of Sample CEBs, 1984

Sample CEBs by location	CEB code number	Rank of sector where CEB located	Group age (years)	Group size (members)	Response rate
Santo Amaro					
Middle-class:	CEB 1-1	5	2	13	100
	1-2	5	9	18	45
	1-3	5	2	35	26
Lower-class:	CEB 1-4	8	17	23	94
	1-5	8	9	15	90
	1-6	8	13	37	68
	1-7	8	5	17	84
	1-8	8	15	45	21
Sé					
Middle-class:	CEB 2-1	1	13	22	60
	2-2	1	9	13	75
	2-3	1	10	13	88
	2-4	1	4	20	
Lower-class:	CEB 2-5	4	2	5	100
	2-6	4	1	5	100
São Miguel					
Middle-class:	CEB 3-1	6	3	12	86
	3-2	6	5	25	90
	3-3	6	6	10	89
	3-4	6	5	15	100
Lower-class:	CEB 3-5	8	2	45	90
	3-6	8	2	25	48
	3-7	8	4	45	37
	3-8	8	3	30	77

Data collection and analysis

In the field, data were collected from a variety of sources using a number of methods. During the initial phase of the research, conducted in 1984, in-depth interviews were conducted with the local archbishop, Dom Paulo Arns, and the auxiliary bishops residing in each of the nine episcopal regions of São Paulo. These were carried out using a prepared question guide that solicited information on their personal background as well as their views on the Church and the CEB phenomenon in general (see Schedule

Table 10. Basic Characteristics of Sample CEBS, 1988

Sample CEBS by location	CEB code number	Rank of sector where CEB located	Group age (years)	Group size (members)	Response rate
Santo Amaro					
Middle-class:	CEB 1-1	5	6	13	
	1-2	5	13	12	
	1-3	5	6	20	
Lower-class:	CEB 1-4	8	21	30	100
	1-5	8	13	20	50
	1-6	8	17	50	29
	1-7	8	9	25	35
	1-8	8	19	20	50
Sé					
Middle-class:	CEB 2-1	1	17	20	
	2-2	1	13	10	
	2-3	1	14	20	
	2-4	1	7	20	
Lower-class:	CEB 2-5	4	6	5	
	2-6	Disbanded			
São Miguel					
Middle-class:	CEB 3-1	6	7	15	
	3-2	6	9	20	
	3-3	6	10	7	
	3-4	Disbanded			
Lower-class:	CEB 3-5	8	6	20	71
	3-6	8	6	20	55
	3-7	8	8	15	36
	3-8	8	7	8	

A). During visits to the central and regional curiae, moreover, available CEB-related documents were also collected and examined.

At the parish level, we used the same question guide to obtain information on pastors and Church agents working with or responsible for specific sample CEBS. To parish pastors, in particular, a few additional questions were directed regarding the size and population of their parishes, the number of CEBS currently in operation, and the groups' ages. Locally produced CEB materials were also requested where they were found to exist.

Aside from offering help in the group-selection process, pastors also lent invaluable assistance by helping me to establish contact with individual CEBs. Their aid, in fact, was crucial to the successful completion of the study for two reasons. On the one hand, it was invariably the case that only the local priest actually knew where the CEBs in his parish were situated when they met, who was in charge, and so forth. On the other hand, when the pastor himself introduced me to a particular CEB, a smoother and speedier entry was nearly always assured. As was learned from experience, CEB participants were more likely to welcome and accept outsiders when they had been cleared by the ranking Church official in the area.

At the CEB level, data were gathered in three ways. First of all, self-identified lay leaders were questioned about the basic features, history, function, and principal activities of their CEB. Here again, a question guide was used, a translation of which is appended as Schedule B.

Second, using a self-administered written questionnaire (see Schedule C), background information was obtained on both CEB leaders and ordinary participants themselves, as well as their opinions on secular and Church-related matters. After regular group meetings or, sometimes celebrações, if necessary, group participants were asked to take a questionnaire, fill it in, and return it to me in one to two weeks' time. To ensure the best possible response rate, I offered a nominal monetary donation (200 to 250 Brazilian cruzeiros, or about 25 U.S. cents) to the CEB for every completed form returned. For the most part, nonresponse was not a problem, and of the 400 questionnaires distributed, some 275, or nearly 70 percent, were returned. Though some fluctuations in response rates between individual CEBs were apparent (see Table 9), these did not seem to vary by region or social class.

The final data-gathering technique employed at the CEB level was participant observation. During the week I spent in each group, I was, in fact, able to collect a good deal of information informally through conversations with ordinary members and attendance at CEB functions.

During the second field-research trip to São Paulo in 1988, this methodology was replicated, using the same groups as in 1984 (minus two that had disbanded), although on a more limited scale. While pastoral agents and group leaders were once again sought out and questioned about changes occurring in the Church and group life, members of the upper hierarchy (with the exception of the bishop responsible for the CEBs, Dom Fernando Penteado) were not reinterviewed. Similarly, though participant observation and self-administered questionnaires were also again employed to examine member attitudes and behavior, not all CEB members were contacted. Because I had decided that the focus of 1988 investigation would be those groups most actively involved in the community-action projects, or revindicações, only their members were subjected to intense reexamination. In addition, the questionnaire used in 1988 was a shortened and revised version of the one employed previously (see Schedule D).

Schedule A
Question guide—hierarchy (1984 and 1988)

1. What is your nationality? 1. Brazilian   2. Other
2. If born outside Brazil, how long have you lived here?
   ____ years   ____ months
3. If Brazilian, in what state were you born?
4. Were you born in a rural or urban area? 1. Rural   2. Urban
5. What was your father's occupation?
6. What is your age? ____ years
7. How long have you been a priest/bishop? ____ years
8. Do you belong to a religious order?
9. How long have you been in this particular parish/region?
   ____ years   ____ months
10. Educational history:
    a) universities attended and level obtained
    b) seminaries attended
11. Professional/career history:
    Place ____ Position ____   Duration ____
12. How would you define a CEB?
13. What do you feel is their role within the Church?
14. What do you feel is their role within society?
15. A great deal of emphasis has been placed on the CEBs within the archdiocesan Pastoral Plan. How would you rate the growth of CEBs in your particular region/parish? 1. Excellent   2. Very good
    3. Good   4. Satisfactory   5. Poor   6. Very poor   Comments
16. What concrete actions have you taken in support of the CEB phenomenon in your region/parish?
17. What difficulties have you encountered in carrying out the Pastoral Plan as it pertains to CEBs?

Schedule B
Question guide—CEB leadership (1984 and 1988)

1. How many people belong to this group?
2. How long has this group been meeting? ____ years   ____ months
3. Why was this group originally formed? 1. To resolve a specific problem in the community   2. To satisfy members' religious needs   3. Other
4. Who initiated this group? 1. Was initiated at the behest of the priest or other Church personnel   2. Emerged spontaneously among the members themselves   3. Other
5. What is the overall function or goal of this group?
6. Which of the following activities does this group participate in? (Possible responses: 1. Regularly   2. Occasionally   3. Rarely   4. Never)
   a) Preparation of the mass, liturgy
   b) Preparation of other sacraments (specify which)
   c) Reflection and discussion
   d) Charity or community work
   e) Political or social consciousness raising
   f) Bible study
   g) Other (Including *revindicações*)
7. How frequently does this group meet? 1. More than once a week   2. Once a week   3. A few times a month   4. Once a month   5. Other
8. Where does this group usually meet? 1. In a church   2. At someone's home   3. Other
9. What is the usual format of meetings?
10. How is this group led? Who directs this group? 1. Priest   2. Nun   3. Priest and nun   4. Layperson or laypersons   5. Priest and layperson   6. Nun and layperson   7. Priest, nun, and laypersons
11. For the most part, who decides what activities will be undertaken by this group? 1. The leaders only   2. The leaders in consultation with the members   3. The leaders and the members all together   4. The members only   5. Other
12. What formal or informal ties does this group have with other groups?
13. Has this group ever sent representatives to regional or national conferences sponsored by the Church? (specify)

Schedule C
CEB member questionnaire (1984)

Preamble

The following questionnaire was formulated to obtain information about the characteristics and attitudes of the members of this and other similar groups. The information obtained will be used in a doctoral dissertation about basic Christian communities of the Catholic Church in Greater São Paulo. Although not specifically intended for publication, parts of this study may appear in books or articles for academic use.

Do not put your name on the questionnaire. The questionnaire must be completed anonymously. Your identity will not be connected in any way with the responses given here.

Please read and respond to each question as best you can, in conformity with the instructions (given orally). In some questions, we seek personal information, or that pertaining to your experience in this group. In others, we seek only your opinion. If there are some questions to which you do not have an answer, or to which you do not wish to respond, feel free to ignore them. Thank you very much for your help.

Part I—Personal background

1. Your age? ____ years
2. Your sex? 1. Male   2. Female
3. Your nationality? 1. Brazilian   2. Other (specify)
4. If Brazilian, in what state were you born? 1. São Paulo   2. Other (specify)
5. If Brazilian, were you born in an urban or rural area? 1. Urban 2. Rural   3. Don't know/don't remember
6. Are you married? 1. Yes   2. No   3. Separated or divorced 4. Don't know/don't remember
7. Are you presently employed? 1. Yes   2. No
8. If you are not presently employed, why not? 1. Student   2. Retired 3. Laid-off   4. Housewife   5. Illness   6. Self-supporting   7. Other (specify)
9. What is your occupation, or was your occupation if not presently employed? If a housewife, what is or was your husband's occupation?

10. More or less, how much does *your family* earn per month? 1. Less than 1 minimum salary   2. Between 1 and 2 MS   3. Between 2 and 5 MS   4. Between 5 and 10 MS   5. Between 10 and 15 MS   6. More than 15 MS   7. Don't know/don't remember

11. Up to what educational level have you completed? 1. Less than elementary   2. Elementary   3. Some secondary   4. Secondary 5. Technical course incomplete   6. Technical course complete 7. University incomplete   8. University level or higher

12. Presently, do you live: 1. In this neighborhood.   2. In another area of the city (specify)

Part II—Religious and secular attitudes and behavior

13. Do you attend mass? 1. More than once a week   2. Once a week 3. A few times per month   4. Once a month   5. A few times a year 6. Never or almost never   7. Don't know/don't remember

14. How often do you pray to each of the following? (Possible responses: 1. Regularly   2. Sometimes   3. Almost never or never 4. Don't know/don't remember)
    a) Our Lady
    b) God
    c) Your devotional saint
    d) The souls
    e) Jesus Christ
    f) Other (specify)

15. Do you visit a spiritist temple? 1. Regularly   2. Sometimes 3. Have visited once or twice   4. Never   5. Don't know/don't remember

16. How would you describe Jesus Christ? (Select the one response which you feel is best) 1. An all-powerful saint   2. The Son of God who was crucified   3. The liberator of the poor and oppressed 4. A great prophet   5. Other (specify)   6. Don't know

17. What does the Catholic Church mean to you? (Select the one response which you feel is best) 1. A place where people pray and receive the sacraments   2. A community of the people of God 3. The priest and the bishops   4. The reunion of baptized souls 5. Other (specify)   6. Don't know

18. To what extent do you trust the following groups to defend the interests of people such as yourself? (Possible responses: 1. A good deal   2. More or less   3. A little   4. Not at all   5. Don't know

a) Unions
b) Government
c) The Catholic Church
d) The Armed Forces
e) Politicians
f) Other (specify)

19. Which of the following problems do you think the Catholic Church can resolve? (Possible responses: 1. Yes   2. Sometimes   3. No   4. Don't know)
    a) Material problems (food, lodging, unemployment)
    b) Crises of faith, spiritual problems
    c) Injustice, transgression of civil and human rights
    d) Personal problems
    e) Other (specify)

20. Which political party (legal or illegal) is closest to your way of thinking? 1. PDS   2. PMDB   3. PT   4. PTB   5. PDT   6. Other (specify)   7. Don't know

21. Aside from political parties, are there other groups or organizations which are close to your way of thinking? (specify)

22. How would you describe your political ideology? 1. Radical left   2. Left   3. Center-left   4. Center   5. Center-right   6. Right   7. Radical right   8. Don't know

23. In the last 5 years, have you participated in any groups connected with the Church, aside from this group? (e.g. devotional groups, Catholic schools, orphanages, etc.)

24. In the last 5 years, have you participated in any secular group or activities? (e.g. neighborhood associations, unions, cultural or professional associations, etc.): _____

Part III—Group-related attitudes and behavior

25. For how long have you been affiliated with this group? _____ years

26. Do you attend the meetings of this group: 1. Regularly   2. Once in a while   3. I have attended once or twice   4. Almost never or never   5. Don't know/don't remember

27. How did you enter the group? 1. Invited by a friend or relative   2. Suggestion of priest, nun, or bishop   3. Approached the group myself and asked to become a member   4. Other (specify)   5. Don't know/don't remember

28. In your decision to join the group, to what extent were the following

factors important? (Possible responses: 1. Important   2. More or less important   3. Not important   4. Don't know/don't remember)
a) Desire to help others
b) Desire to enhance personal faith
c) Desire for greater human contact
d) Looking for an objective in life
e) Other (specify)

29. Since joining the group, has your life changed in any of the following ways? (Possible responses: 1. Enhanced   2. Diminished   3. Continues the same   4. Don't know)
a) Relationship with the Catholic Church
b) Relationship with your family
c) Interest in the problems of others
d) Consciousness of social or political problems
e) Other (specify)

30. Before you joined this group, how many of its members did you know already? 1. All or nearly all the members   2. Some members   3. None or almost none of the members   4. Don't know/don't remember

31. If you knew all or almost all of the members before joining, how did you know them? 1. We lived in the same neighborhood   2. We felt the same religious necessities   3. We confronted the same socioeconomic problems   4. Other (specify)   5. Don't know/don't remember

32. In your opinion, what are the most serious problems confronting people like yourself?

33. Since entering this group, has your consciousness of these problems (referring to Question 32) increased? 1. A lot   2. More or less   3. A little   4. Not at all   5. Don't know

34. Has the group offered you an opportunity to help resolve these problems (referring to Question 32)? 1. A lot   2. More or less   3. A little   4. Not at all   5. Don't know

35. What do you think is the principal function of this group?

36. How would you describe the commitment of ordinary members to this purpose (referring to Question 35) as compared to the commitment of group leaders? 1. The members are more committed than the leaders   2. The leaders are more committed than the members   3. The leaders and members are equally committed   4. Don't know

37. As a member of this group, how often do you normally participate in the following activities? (Possible responses: 1. Regularly 2. Sometimes   3. Almost never or never   4. Not a group activity 5. Don't know/don't remember)
    a) Preparation for the mass, or other sacraments
    b) Reflection and discussion
    c) Charity work or community assistance
    d) Political or social consciousness-raising
    e) Bible study to enhance faith
    f) Other (specify)

38. Upon which of these activities (referring to Question 37) would you like to see the group place *more* emphasis? 1. Preparation of mass or other sacraments   2. Reflection and discussion   3. Charity or community work   4. Social or political consciousness-raising 5. Bible study to enhance faith   6. Other (specify)   7. All activities are satisfactorily emphasized within this group   8. Don't know

39. Upon which of these activities (referring to Question 37) would you like to see the group place *less* emphasis? 1. Preparation of mass or other sacraments   2. Reflection and discussion   3. Charity or community work   4. Social or political consciousness-raising 5. Bible study to enhance faith   6. Other (specify)   7. All activities are satisfactorily emphasized within this group   8. Don't know

40. Who decides what activities will be undertaken by this group?
    1. Only the leaders   2. Only the ordinary members   3. The leaders after consulting the members   4. The leaders and the members all together   5. Other (specify)   6. Don't know

41. How often do you participate in decision-making within this group?
    1. Regularly   2. Sometimes   3. Almost never   4. Not at all 5. Don't know/don't remember

42. In terms of its ability to achieve its objectives, how would you evaluate the organization of this group? 1. Well organized 2. Organized satisfactorily   3. Poorly organized   4. Don't know

43. How would you compare the present organization of this group with the way it was organized when you first joined? 1. Now better 2. Now worse   3. The same   4. Don't know

44. Do you own the home in which you live? 1. Yes   2. No 3. Don't know

45. Group coordinator or *conselho* member? 1. Yes   2. No

46. Comments

Schedule D
CEB member questionnaire (1988)

Preamble

The following questionnaire was formulated to obtain information about the characteristics and attitudes of the members of this group, and of other similar groups. The information obtained will be used to complete a study of lay groups in São Paulo initiated in 1984. A part or parts of this study may be published for academic use in book or article form.

Do not put your name on the questionnaire. The questionnaire must be completed anonymously. Your identity will not be connected in any way with the responses given here.

Please read and respond to each question as best you can, in comformity with the instructions. In some questions, we solicit personal information, or about your experience in this group. In others, we solicit only your opinion. If you encounter a question to which you do not wish to respond, feel free to ignore it.

Thank you very much for your help.

Part I—Group-related attitudes and behavior

1. How long have you been affiliated with this group? ＿＿ years.
2. How often do you attend group meetings? 1. Regularly
   2. Sometimes   3. I have attended once or twice
3. Since you joined the group, has your life changed in any of the following ways? (Possible responses: 1. Enhanced   2. Same
   3. Diminished)
   a) Relationship with the Catholic Church
   b) Family relationship
   c) Consciousness of social/political problems
   d) Other
4. In your opinion, what are the gravest problems facing people like you?
5. Since you joined the group, has your consciousness of these problems increased? 1. Yes   2. More or less   3. No
6. Has this group offered you an opportunity to resolve these problems? 1. Yes   2. More or less   3. No
7. As a member of this group, how often do you normally participate in the following activities? (Possible responses: 1. Regularly

2. Sometimes   3. Never   4. Not a group activity)
a) Preparation of the mass
b) Preparation of the sacraments
c) Reflection
d) Charity or community assistance
e) Social or political consciousness raising
f) Community action projects
g) Other

8. Are you a member of the council or leadership of this group? 1. Yes
2. No

Part II—Religious and secular attitudes and behavior

9. Do you attend mass? 1. More than once a week   2. Once a week
3. A few times a month   4. Once a month   5. A few times a year
6. Almost never or never

10. How would you describe Jesus Christ? (Possible responses: 1. Yes
2. No)
a) An all-powerful saint
b) The Son of God who was crucified
c) Liberator of the poor and oppressed
d) A great prophet
e) Other

11. To defend the interests of people like you, how much do you confide
in the following groups? (Possible responses: 1. Very much   2. More
or less   3. Little)
a) Unions
b) Governments
c) Catholic Church
d) Armed Forces
e) Politicians
f) Other

12. Do you trust in the Catholic Church to resolve: (Possible responses:
1. Very much   2. More or less   3. Little)
a) Material problems (food, shelter, employment)
b) Crises of faith
c) Social injustice
d) Personal problems
e) Other

13. Which of the political parties best expresses your way of thinking?
    1. PDS   2. PMDB   3. PT   4. PFL   5. PDT   6. PTB   7. Other
14. In the last five years, have you participated in any civic associations or groups? (eg. neighborhood associations, unions, cultural and professional associations, etc.)?

Part III—Personal background questions

15. Your age? _____ years
16. Your sex? 1. Male   2. Female
17. In what state were you born? 1. São Paulo   2. Other
18. Were you born in an urban or rural area? 1. Urban   2. Rural
19. How long have you lived here in the city of São Paulo? _____ years
20. Are you married? 1. Married   2. Single   3. Separated or divorced   4. Widowed
21. Are you presently employed? 1. Yes   2. No
22. If you are not presently employed, why not? 1. Student   2. Retired   3. Laid-off   4. Housewife   5. Illness   6. Other
23. What is your occupation, or was your occupation if not presently employed? If a housewife, what is your husband's occupation?
24. More or less, how much does *your family* earn per month? 1. Less than 1 minimum salary   2. Between 1 and 2 MS   3. Between 2 and 5 MS   4. Between 5 and 10 MS   5. Between 10 and 15 MS   6. More than 15 MS   7. Don't know
25. Up to what educational level have you completed? 1. Less than elementary   2. Elementary   3. Some secondary   4. Secondary   5. Technical course incomplete   6. Technical course complete   7. University incomplete   8. University level or higher
26. Do you live in: 1. Your own house   2. Rented house

Notes

Introduction

1 See W. W. Rostow, "The Take-Off into Self-Sustained Growth." *Economic Journal,* March 1956, pp. 26–48.

2 See Karl Marx, "On the Jewish Question," in *Karl Marx: Early Writings,* ed. T. B. Bottomore (London: C. A. Watts, 1963), pp. 3–40; and Karl Marx, "Theses on Feuerbach," in *Marx and Engels: Basic Writings on Politics and Philosophy,* ed. Lewis S. Feuer (Garden City, N.J.: Anchor, 1959), pp. 243–48.

3 The most recent critique of the literature on development and underdevelopment is Robert G. Gilpin, "Development and Underdevelopment: Conflicting Perspectives on the Third World," in *Philosophy, History and Social Action,* ed. Sidney Hook, William L. O'Neill, and Roger O'Toole (Dordrecht, Boston, and London: Kluwer Academic Publishers, 1988), pp. 173–208.

4 This discussion is based on examinations of Gramsci's work contained in James A. Beckford, "Quasi-Marxisms and the Sociology of Religion" (Paper presented at the Annual Meeting of the Society for the Scientific Study of Religion, Chicago, 28–30 October 1988); and in John Fulton, "Religion and Politics in Gramsci: An Introduction," *Sociological Analysis* 48, no. 3 (1987): 197–216.

5 Otto Maduro, *Religion and Social Conflicts,* trans. Robert R. Barr (Maryknoll, N.Y.: Orbis, 1982); Otto Maduro, "Catholic Church, State Power, and Popular Movements" (Paper presented at the Annual Meeting of the Society for the Scientific Study of Religion, Providence, R.I., 21–24 October 1982).

6 See H. H. Gerth and C. Wright Mills, eds., *From Max Weber: Essays in Sociology* (New York: Oxford University Press, 1946), p. 268.

7 There are a number of excellent works dealing with the subject of liberation theology. Among the better overviews are Deane W. Ferm, *Third World Liberation Theologies* (Maryknoll, N.Y.: Orbis, 1986); Edward Cleary, *Crisis and Change: The Church in Latin America Today* (Maryknoll, N.Y.: Orbis, 1985); and Richard Rubenstein and John Roth, eds., *The Political Significance of Latin American Liberation Theology* (Washington, D.C.: Washington Institute Press, 1988).

8 See Alvaro Barreiro, *Basic Ecclesial Communities,* trans. Barbara Campbell (Mary-

knoll, N.Y.: Orbis, 1982); Frei Betto, *O que é comunidade eclesial de base?* (São Paulo: Brasiliense, 1981), and "As comunidades eclesiais de base como potencial de transformação da sociedade Brasileira," *Revista eclesiástica Brasileira* 43 (September 1983): 494–503; Leonardo Boff, "Theological Characteristics of a Grassroots Church," in *The Challenge of Basic Christian Communities*, ed. Sergio Torres and John Eagleson, trans. John Drury (Maryknoll, N.Y.: Orbis, 1981), pp. 124–44; and Leonardo Boff, "CEBs: A Igreja inteira na base," *Revista eclesiástica Brasileira* 43 (September 1983): 459–69.

9   Daniel H. Levine, "Popular Groups, Popular Culture, and Popular Religion," Working Paper No. 127, Helen Kellogg Institute for International Studies, University of Notre Dame, Notre Dame, Indiana (August 1989); Scott Mainwaring, "Grassroots Catholic Groups and Politics in Brazil," in *The Progressive Church in Latin America*, ed. Scott Mainwaring and Alexander Wilde (Notre Dame: University of Notre Dame Press, 1989).

10 See Conferência Nacional dos Bispos do Brasil (CNBB), *Comunidades eclesiais de base na Igreja do Brasil* (São Paulo: Paulinas, 1983), p. 13.

11 Mariano Baraglia, *Evolução das comunidades eclesiais de base* (Petrópolis, RJ.: Vozes, 1974), p. 42.

12 Daniel H. Levine, "Popular Groups and Popular Culture" (Paper presented at the Annual Meeting of the Society for the Scientific Study of Religion, Chicago, 28–30 October 1988); Ivo Follmann, *Igreja, ideologia, e classes sociais* (Petrópolis, RJ.: Vozes, 1985), pt. 3.

13 Marcello de C. Azevedo, *Basic Ecclesial Communities in Brazil: The Challenge of a New Way of Being Church* (Washington, D.C.: Georgetown University Press, 1987), chap. 2.

14 See Follmann, *Igreja, ideologia, e classes sociais*, p. 173.

15 Barreiro, *Basic Ecclesial Communities*, p. 2. This study was originally published in Portuguese in 1977.

16 See Betto, *O que é comunidade*, p. 17; Irmão Michel, "Comunidades Católicas de base são o fruto de colaboração entre duas classes sociais, a pobre e a média," *Revista eclesiástica Brasileira* 42 (March 1982): 121; and Thomas G. Sanders, "The Catholic Church in Brazil's Political Transition," *American Universities Field Staff Reports* 48 (1980).

17 Gottfried Deelen, "The Church on Its Way to the People: Basic Christian Communities in Brazil," *Cross Currents* 30 (1980): 385; Thomas C. Bruneau, "Basic Christian Communities in Latin America: Their Nature and Significance (Especially in Brazil)," in *Churches and Politics in Latin America*, ed. Daniel H. Levine (Beverly Hills, Calif.: Sage, 1979), p. 225; Pedro A. Ribeiro de Oliveira, "Oprimidos: A opção pela Igreja," *Revista eclesiástica Brasileira* 41 (December 1981): 643; Adelina Baldissera, *CEBs: Poder, nova sociedade* (São Paulo: Paulinas, 1988), p. 60; and Dom Amaury Castanho, "Caminho das CEBs no Brasil," *Revista eclesiástica Brasileira* 46 (September 1986): 663.

18 As cited in Baldissera, *CEBs: Poder, nova sociedade*, p. 60.

19 Betto, *O que é comunidade?* p. 17.

20 As cited in Baldissera, *CEBs: Poder, nova sociedade*, p. 60.

21 Cleary, *Crisis and Change*, p. 104.

22 See Afonso Gregory, "Dados préliminares sobre experiências de comunidades eclesiais de base no Brasil," in *Comunidades eclesiais de base: Utopia ou realidade?* ed. Afonso

Gregory (Petrópolis, RJ.: Vozes, 1973); and Pedro Demo and Elizeu F. Calsing, "Relatório da pesquisa sobre CEBs," in Conferência Nacional dos Bispos do Brasil (CNBB),
Comunidades: Igreja na base (São Paulo: Paulinas, 1977), pp. 13–64.

23 Clodovis Boff, "Em que ponto estão hoje as CEBs?" *Revista eclesiástica Brasileira* 46
(September 1986): 527–38.

24 The data presented here are derived from a study conducted in 1982 by the Grupo de
Estudos sobre Partidos, Eleições e Problemas Institucionais of the Associação Nacional
de Programas de Pesquisa e Pós-graduação em Ciências Sociais, in conjunction with
the Instituto Universitário de Pesquisas do Rio de Janeiro.

25 Thomas C. Bruneau, *The Church in Brazil* (Austin: University of Texas Press, 1982).

26 Personal communication with Pedro A. Ribeiro de Oliveira, 29 October 1988, Chicago.

27 See Oliveira, "Oprimidos," p. 651.

1 The Origins of Church Innovation

1 On the recent history of the Latin American Catholic Church, see Daniel H. Levine,
ed., *Churches and Politics in Latin America* (Beverly Hills, Calif.: Sage, 1979); and
Scott Mainwaring and Alexander Wilde, eds., *The Progressive Church in Latin America*
(Notre Dame: University of Notre Dame Press, 1989).

2 See Thomas C. Bruneau, *The Political Transformation of the Brazilian Catholic Church*
(London: Cambridge University Press, 1974), pp. 16–50.

3 Conferência Nacional dos Bispos do Brasil (CNBB), *Diretrizes gerais da ação pastoral
da Igreja no Brasil, 1987–1990* (São Paulo: Paulinas, 1983), p. 35.

4 Conferência Nacional dos Bispos do Brasil (CNBB), *Igreja no Brasil, 1984.* (Brasilia:
CNBB, 1984), p. 95.

5 Instituto Brasileiro de Geografia e Estatística (IBGE), *Anuário estatístico do Brasil.* (Rio
de Janeiro: Fundação IBGE, 1982), pp. 120, 196.

6 On this process, see Madeleine Adriance, *Opting for the Poor: Brazilian Catholicism
in Transition* (Kansas City, Mo.: Sheed and Ward, 1986), chaps. 4, 6.

7 The nature and impact of the military coup has been described by a number of authors,
including Barry Ames, *Rhetoric and Reality in a Militarized Regime: Brazil since 1964*
(Beverly Hills, Calif.: Sage, 1973); Kenneth Erickson, *The Brazilian Corporative State
and Working-Class Politics* (Berkeley: University of California Press, 1977); Peter Flynn,
Brazil: A Political Analysis (London: Ernest Benn, 1978); and Alfred Stepan, ed., *Authoritarian Brazil* (New Haven: Yale University Press, 1973).

8 See Rowan Ireland, "Catholic Base Communities, Spiritist Groups, and the Deepening
of Democracy in Brazil," in *The Progressive Church in Latin America*, ed. Scott Mainwaring and Alexander Wilde (Notre Dame: University of Notre Dame Press, 1989), pp.
224–50.

9 See Comissão Arquidiocesana de Pastoral dos Direitos Humanos e Marginalizados de
São Paulo (CAPDH), *Fé e política* (Petrópolis, RJ.: Vozes, 1981), p. 94.

10 Brazilian Catholic Action was first established in 1935, as part of an international lay
movement oriented toward promoting the faith. In the 1950s, it was reorganized, however, along European lines, and directed its evangelizing activities to specific sectors
of the Brazilian population. See Bruneau, *The Political Transformation*, pp. 45, 94–

95; and Romeu Dale, "Da Ação Católica à opção pelos pobres," *SEDOC* 12 (May 1980): 1127.

11 For an overview of the development and impact of other progressive programs sponsored by the Church in the diocese of Natal during this period, see Cândido Procópio Ferreira de Camargo, *Igreja e desenvolvimento* (São Paulo: Editora Brasileira de Ciências, 1971).

12 See Bruneau, *The Political Transformation*, pp. 80–85; and Dale, "Da Ação Católica," p. 1127.

13 See CAPDH, *Fé e política*, pp. 96–98.

14 See Riordan Roett, *Brazil: Politics in a Patrimonial State* (Boston: Allyn and Bacon, 1972), pp. 118–19; and Charles Antoine, *Church and Power in Brazil*, trans. Peter Nelson (London: Sheed and Ward, 1973), p. 15.

15 See CAPDH, *Fé e política*, pp. 114–16.

16 For a discussion of these materials, see Thomas C. Bruneau, "Church and Politics in Brazil: The Genesis of Change," *Journal of Latin American Studies* 17 (1985): 276–77.

17 See CAPDH, *Fé e política*, pp. 110–12.

18 Vanilda Paiva, "A Igreja moderna no Brasil," in *Igreja e questão agrária*, ed. Vanilda Paiva (São Paulo: Loyola, 1985), pp. 52–67.

19 Roberto Romano, *Brasil: Igreja contra Estado* (São Paulo: Kairós Livraria e Editora, 1979).

20 Ivan Vallier, "Religious Elites: Differentiations and Developments in Roman Catholicism," in *Elites in Latin America*, ed. Seymour Martin Lipset and Aldo Solari (New York: Oxford University Press, 1967), pp. 190–232.

21 Ralph Della Cava, "Igreja e Estado no Brasil do Século XX: Sete monografias recentes sobre o Catolicismo Brasileiro, 1916–64," *Estudos CEBRAP* 12 (April–June 1975): 5–52.

22 For the most recent version of his argument, see Bruneau, "Church and Politics in Brazil."

23 Bruneau, "Church and Politics in Brazil," p. 286.

24 Enrique Dussel, "Current Events in Latin America (1972–1980)," in *The Challenge of Basic Christian Communities*, ed. Torres and Eagleson, p. 100.

25 Gustavo Gutiérrez, "The Irruption of the Poor in Latin America and the Christian Communities of the Common People," in *The Challenge of Basic Christian Communities*, ed. Torres and Eagleson, pp. 108–9.

26 Leonardo Boff, "Theological Characteristics of a Grassroots Church," in *The Challenge of Basic Christian Communities*, ed. Torres and Eagleson, p. 128.

27 Maduro, *Religion and Social Conflicts* and "Catholic Church, State Power, and Popular Movements."

28 See Luiz Gonzaga de Souza Lima, *Evolução política dos Católicos e da Igreja no Brasil* (Petrópolis, RJ.: Vozes, 1979), pp. 30–40; Scott Mainwaring, *The Catholic Church and Politics in Brazil, 1916–1985* (Stanford: Stanford University Press, 1986), pp. 14–17, chap. 9; and Adriance, *Opting for the Poor*, pp. 106–25.

29 See, for example, Azevedo, *Basic Ecclesial Communities in Brazil*; Barreiro, *Basic Ecclesial Communities*; Bruneau, *The Church in Brazil*; and Dom Luis Gonzaga Fernandes, "Gênese, dinâmica e perspectiva das CEBs do Brasil," *Revista eclesiástica Brasileira* 42 (September 1982): 456–64.

30 See Sylvia Hewlett, *The Cruel Dilemmas of Development: Twentieth Century Brazil* (New York: Basic Books, 1980), pp. 36–56.
31 CNBB, *Comunidades eclesiais de base*, pp. 5, 12.

2 Innovation in the Archdiocese of São Paulo

1 Empresa Metropolitana de Planejamento da Grande São Paulo (EMPLASA), *Sumário de dados da grande São Paulo* (São Paulo: EMPLASA, 1985), pp. 78, 157.
2 EMPLASA, *Sumário de dados* (1982), p. 90.
3 The monthly minimum salary has historically fluctuated around the U.S. $50 level. It should be noted as well that incomes in Brazil are typically expressed as multiples of the monthly minimum salary.
4 EMPLASA, *Sumário de dados* (1985), p. 97.
5 Between 1970 and 1980, the Brazilian economy grew by some 5 percent to 10 percent annually. Since 1981, however, it has been shrinking. The growth rate for 1981 was −1.6 percent; for 1982, 0.9 percent; and for 1983, −3.2 percent. Some recovery has occurred since 1984. In that year, the economy grew by an estimated 4.2 percent. See EMPLASA, *Sumário de dados* (1985), p. 79. Such poor economic performance has been attributed to a combination of factors, including fluctuations in the price of commodity exports, rising costs of imports such as crude oil, a crushing foreign debt of over U.S. $100 billion, and the very uneven attempts of the Brazilian government to control spending.
6 In 1984, for example, official estimates, determined by the Instituto Brasileiro de Geografia e Estatística (IBGE), put unemployment in the region at 7 percent to 8 percent of the work force. Yet, two other studies, one conducted by SEADE (São Paulo state's statistical body), and the other by DIEESE (a fact-finding body connected with the labor unions), showed the actual unemployment rate to be closer to 15 percent. See "Pesquisa mostra desemprego de 15 percento em São Paulo," *Folha de São Paulo*, 25 May 1984, p. 8.
7 See "A perda dos salários," *Folha de São Paulo*, 1 June 1988, p. A22; and "Fipe aponta desaceleração na alta do custo de vida em S.P." *Folha de São Paulo*, 1 June 1988, p. A32.
8 Governo do Estado de São Paulo (GESP), *Subdivisão do município de São Paulo em áreas homogênias* (São Paulo: Secretaria de Economia e Planejamento, Governo do Estado de São Paulo, 1977), pp. 5–7; EMPLASA, *Sumário de dados* (1985), pp. 44, 74.
9 Instituto Brasileiro de Geografia e Estatística (IBGE), *IX recenseamento geral do Brasil, 1980*, vol. 4, no. 19 (Rio de Janeiro: FIBGE, 1980), pp. 477, 484.
10 EMPLASA, *Sumário de dados* (1985), p. 74.
11 IBGE, *IX recenseamento geral do Brasil, 1980*, vol. 6, no. 19 (Rio de Janeiro: FIBGE, 1980), p. 88.
12 Pontifícia Comissão Justiça e Paz (PCJP), *São Paulo: Growth and Poverty* (London: Bowerdean Press, 1978), p. 41.
13 IBGE, *IX recenseamento geral do Brasil, 1980*, vol. 6, no. 19, p. 184.
14 PCJP, *São Paulo: Growth and Poverty*, p. 32.
15 "Criminalidade aumenta, como era de se esperar," *Folha de São Paulo*, 28 May 1984, p. 12.
16 EMPLASA, *Sumário de dados* (1985), pp. 74, 290.
17 EMPLASA, *Sumário de dados* (1985), pp. 74, 299.

18 EMPLASA, *Sumário de dados* (1985), p. 313.

19 PCJP, *São Paulo: Growth and Poverty*, pp. 35–36.

20 Data on the Church and Church personnel are taken from Archdiocese of São Paulo, *Guia geral da arquidiocese de São Paulo, 1983* (São Paulo: Archdiocese of São Paulo, 1983), and *5º plano de pastoral, 1987–1990*, doc. 3 (São Paulo: Archdiocese of São Paulo, 1987).

21 By papal decree, the archdiocese of São Paulo was reduced in March 1989 to the central core area of metropolitan São Paulo, and four new dioceses were created: Osasco, Campo Limpo, Santo Amaro, and São Miguel.

22 Paulo Evaristo Cardeal Arns, *Em favor do homem* (Rio de Janeiro: Avenir, 1979), p. 36.

23 Getúlio Bittencourt and Sergio Markum, *Dom Paulo Evaristo Arns: O cardeal do povo* (São Paulo: Alfa-Omega, 1979), p. 16; Mauro Santayana, *No meio do povo—Perfil biográfico de Dom Paulo Evaristo Arns* (São Paulo: Editora Salesiana Dom Bosco, 1983), p. 16.

24 Santayana, *No meio do povo*, p. 16.

25 Bittencourt and Markum, *Dom Paulo Evaristo Arns*, p. 20.

26 Arns, *Em favor do homen*, p. 36.

27 CAPDH, *Fé e política*, p. 118.

28 Arns, *Em favor do homem*, p. 36.

29 Sanders, "The Catholic Church," pp. 13–14.

30 Cláudio Hummes and Frei Betto, "A Igreja e a greve do ABC," *Revista eclesiástica Brasileira* 40 (December 1980): 723.

31 Paulo Evaristo Cardeal Arns, "Entrevista do cardeal de São Paulo ao jornal 'Movimento'" *SEDOC* 12 (June 1980): 1226.

32 Between 1964 and 1985, Brazilian presidents were selected by an electoral college consisting primarily of federal legislators and some representatives from the state assemblies. Because of the large number of political appointees and the government party's strength in the populous rural northeast of Brazil, the college was traditionally stacked in favor of military candidates, who, in any case, customarily ran unopposed.

33 See "Dom Paulo inaugura centro de defesa dos direitos humanos," *Folha de São Paulo*, 19 March 1984, p. 5; and "Dom Paulo reitera apoia à diretas-já," *Folha de São Paulo*, 19 April 1984, p. 6. Unfortunately, all such efforts were unsuccessful, and the next president (Tancredo Neves) was elected in 1985 not by popular vote but by the electoral college. In an ironic twist of fate, Neves died, however, before ever assuming office, and was replaced by his running mate, José Sarney.

34 Arns, *Em favor do homem*, p. 19.

35 Archdiocese of São Paulo, *3º plano bienal de pastoral, 1981–1983* (São Paulo: Archdiocese of São Paulo, 1981), p. 34–35.

36 Quotes cited throughout this section, unless otherwise indicated, are taken from a personal interview with Cardinal Arns conducted in May 1984 in São Paulo.

37 Numbers cited are from Archdiocese of São Paulo, *Guia geral da arquidiocese de São Paulo, 1980* (São Paulo: Archdiocese of São Paulo, 1980); Archdiocese of São Paulo, *Guia geral, 1983*; and raw data made available to the author by the archdiocesan curia in June 1988.

38 A sector typically contains 5 or 6 parishes. Some, however, possess as few as 2, whereas others have as many as 12.

39 Socioeconomic scores were determined using a homogeneous mapping scheme devised by the São Paulo state government; see GESP, *Subdivisão do município de São Paulo*. Pastors ages were calculated from archdiocesan records and from information contained in Centro de Estatística Religiosa e Investigaçoes Sociais (CERIS), *Anuário Católico* (Rio de Janeiro: CERIS, 1977).

3 Functions and Activities

1   A thorough discussion of sampling procedures and research methods and instruments appears in the Appendix.

2   See Heléna Salem, "As comunidades eclesiais, ou re-invenção da Igreja," in *A Igreja dos oprimidos*, ed. Antonio Carlos Moura et al. (São Paulo: Editora Brasil Debates, 1981), pp. 155–65; and Mainwaring, "Grassroots Catholic Groups and Politics in Brazil," pp. 151–92.

3   See Paulo Freire, *The Pedagogy of the Oppressed*, trans. Myra Bergman Ramos (New York: Seabury Press, 1970).

4   On CEB involvement of this type in the city of Vitória, Espírito Santo state, see Ana Maria Doimo, "Social Movements and the Catholic Church in Vitória, Brazil," in *The Progressive Church*, ed. Mainwaring and Wilde, pp. 193–223.

5   Ricardo Galletta et al. eds., *Pastoral popular e política partidária* (São Paulo: Paulinas, 1986), pp. 28–35.

4 Organization, Leadership, and Control

1   Unless otherwise indicated, quotes cited throughout this section are taken from personal interviews with Cardinal Paulo Evaristo Arns conducted in May 1984.

2   Paulo Evaristo Cardeal Arns, "Resposta de Dom Paulo Evaristo, Cardeal Arns, às questões de Claudio Viezzoli e Carlo Tassara, do 'Comitato Internazionale per 1º Sviluppo Dei Popoli,'" *SEDOC* 15 (May 1983): 1131.

3   As quoted in Santayana, *No meio do povo*, p. 32.

4   See "A Palavra de Deus e as comunidades eclesiais de base," joint statement released by the bishops of São Paulo, 1982.

5   Interview with Dom Alfredo Novak, 31 January 1984.

6   Interview with Dom Luciano Mendes de Almeida, 10 March 1984.

7   Interview with Dom Fernando Penteado, 16 February 1984.

8   Interview with Dom Antonio Gaspar, 2 February 1984.

9   Interview with Dom Joel Capatan, 1 February 1984.

10 Bruneau, *The Church in Brazil*, p. 109.

11 Conferência Nacional dos Bispos do Brasil (CNBB), *Comunidades eclesiais de base no Brasil* (São Paulo: Paulinas, 1981), p. 45.

12 Baldissera, *CEBs: Poder, nova sociedade* (São Paulo: Paulinas, 1988), p. 119.

13 These encounters, or *reuniões,* occur fairly frequently, but according to no set schedule; and unfortunately, the Church keeps no precise records of how many are held at any given level during the year. In the archdiocese of São Paulo, the most common type of meeting occurs at the sectoral level, with fewer encounters at higher levels of Church government. At the national level, for example, there have been only about half a dozen

CEB conferences since the first was held in Vitória (Espírito Santo state) in 1976. See Azevedo, *Basic Ecclesial Communities*, p. 99.

14   See Clodovis Boff, "Agente de pastoral e povo," *Revista eclesiástica Brasileira* 40 (June 1980): 216–41.

15   In this regard, Adriance argues that women religious are somewhat more effective in this role than men. See Adriance, *Opting for the Poor*, pp. 117–21; and Adriance, "Opting for the Poor: A Social-Historical Analysis of the Changing Brazilian Catholic Church," *Sociological Analysis* 46 (Summer 1985): 142.

5   Social Location of the Membership

1   See, for example, Karl Mannheim, *Ideology and Utopia* (New York: Harcourt, Brace and World, 1936), pp. 270–76; and Matilda White Riley, "Aging, Social Change and the Power of Ideas," *Daedalus* 107 (Fall 1978): 39–52.

2   Eduardo Hoornaert, "Comunidades de base: Dez anos de experiência," *Revista eclesiástica Brasileira* 38 (September 1978): 474–502.

3   Leonardo Boff as quoted in Sonia Alvarez, "Women's Participation in the 'People's Church': A Critical Appraisal" (Paper presented at the 14th International Congress of the Latin American Studies Association, New Orleans, 17–19 March 1988), pp. 1–2.

4   Shulamit Goldsmit and Ernest S. Sweeney, "The Church and Latin American Women in Their Struggle for Equality and Justice," *Thought* 63 (June 1988): 183.

5   For a description of Catholicism as it has traditionally been practiced in Brazil, see Emanuel de Kadt, *Catholic Radicals in Brazil* (London: Oxford University Press, 1970); Kadt, "Religion, the Church and Social Change in Brazil," in *The Politics of Conformity in Latin America*, ed. Claudio Veliz (London: Oxford University Press, 1967); and Emilio Willems, *Followers of the New Faith* (Nashville: Vanderbilt University Press, 1968).

6   Alvarez, "Women's Participation in the 'People's Church,'" pp. 40–41.

7   See J. B. Libânio, "Igreja: Povo oprimido que se organiza para a libertação," *Revista eclesiástica Brasileira* 41 (June 1981): 303; and Oliveira, "Oprimidos," p. 651.

8   The name Maria Ferreira dos Santos is a pseudonym.

9   See Barreiro, *Basic Ecclesial Communities*, p. 56; and Ireland, "Catholic Base Communities," p. 230.

10   Interview with Cardinal Arns, May 1984.

11   Interview with Dom Angélico Bernardino, 2 March 1984.

12   Bruneau, *The Church in Brazil*, p. 140.

13   The percentages cited in this paragraph do not add up to 100 percent because of missing responses.

14   Equivalent to approximately U.S. $50. Income categories are based on those used by the Instituto Brasileiro de Geografia e Estatística (IBGE).

15   This income spread would likely be greater were it not for problems associated with respondents' underreporting of wages at the upper end of the wage scale. Brazilians, especially those within the middle class, are inclined to understate their earnings— usually in accordance with what they've reported as income to the taxation department. The São Paulo respondents represent no exception to this rule.

6   A Case Study of the Comunidades Santa Heléna and São José

1   The names of CEBs, pastoral agents, and individual members cited in this chapter are pseudonyms.

2   These statistics are for micro-areas of the municipality of São Paulo that were selected to correspond roughly with parish or CEB neighborhood boundaries. These and all other data presented in this chapter that refer to family incomes within specific geographical areas were taken from Prefeitura do Município de São Paulo (PMSP), *Projeção do população do município de São Paulo por micro-área: 7º relatório* (São Paulo: PMSP, Coordenadora Geral de Planejamento, 1980).

7   The Potential for Social Change

1   As Maduro has pointed out, despite recent developments in the Marxist-Christian dialogue, the two sides still tend to reject each other's views. See Maduro, *Religion and Social Conflicts*, p. xxvii.

2   Arns, "Resposta de Dom Paulo," p. 1131.

3   Arns, "Resposta de Dom Paulo," p. 1131.

4   See Barreiro, *Basic Ecclesial Communities*; Betto, *O que é comunidade?*; and Leonardo Boff, "Theological Characteristics of a Grassroots Church."

5   Betto, "As comunidades eclesiais de base como potencial," p. 503.

6   Galletta et al., eds., *Pastoral popular*, p. 28.

7   J. B. Libânio, "CEBs: Igreja em busca da terra prometida," *Revista eclesiástica Brasileira* 46 (September 1986): 489–511.

8   Of all Brazilian liberationists, Clodovis Boff has perhaps been the most consistently outspoken with respect to difficulties encountered by the CEBs. As early as 1979, he identified a number of factors threatening CEB activation—factors originating both within and outside the groups. See Clodovis Boff, "A influência política das comunidades eclesiais de base (CEBs)," *Religião e sociedade* 4 (1979): 95–120; and Clodovis Boff, "Em que ponto estão hoje as CEBs?" *Revista eclesiástica Brasileira* 46 (September 1986): 527–38.

9   Eduardo Hoornaert, "Os três fatores da nova hegemonia dentro da Igreja Católica no Brasil: Fatos e perspectivas," *Revista eclesiástica Brasileira* 26 (June 1986): 371–84.

10   Ireland, "Catholic Base Communities," p. 226.

11   Mainwaring, "Grassroots Catholic Groups and Politics," p. 185.

12   Daniel Levine, "Religion, the Poor, and Politics in Latin America Today," in *Religion and Political Conflict in Latin America*, ed. Daniel H. Levine (Chapel Hill: University of North Carolina Press, 1986), p. 15.

13   See Max Weber, *The Protestant Ethic and the Spirit of Capitalism* (New York: Charles Scribner's Sons, 1958); and Gerth and Mills, eds., *From Max Weber*, chap. 12.

14   Data based on unofficial estimates provided by the Supervisão de Obras Públicas, Regiões Administrativas de Itaquera e Capela do Socorro, Município de São Paulo, June 1988.

15   Taken from EMPLASA, *Sumário de dados*, 1982, 1985, and 1987.

16   See, for example, Roett, *Brazil: Politics in a Patrimonial State*.

17   For a thorough discussion of patron-clientelism in Brazil, see Emanuel de Kadt, *Catholic*

Radicals in Brazil (London: Oxford University Press, 1970). For an examination of how patron-clientelism operates at the level of urban neighborhoods, see also Robert Gay, "Neighborhood Associations and Political Change in Rio de Janeiro," *Latin American Research Review* 25, no. 1 (1990): 102–18.

18 Alexis de Tocqueville, *Democracy in America*, vol. 2, trans. Henry Reeve (New York: Random House, 1945), pp. 129–32.

19 Interview with Dom Alfredo Novak, 31 January 1984.

20 On the effects of Church constraints on discussion and action, see also Ruth Cardoso, "Duas faces de uma experiência," *Novos estudos CEBRAP* 2 (April 1982): 53–58; and Doimo, "Social Movements and the Catholic Church," pp. 193–223.

21 Interview with Dom Luciano Mendes de Almeida, 10 March 1984.

8 Changes in Direction

1   Interview with Dom Fernando Penteado, 2 June 1988.

2   See Gerth and Mills, eds., *From Max Weber*, chap. 8; and Robert Michels, *Political Parties* (New York: Free Press, 1962).

3   Interview with Dom Fernando Penteado, 2 June 1988.

4   On the origins and scope of Church changes after this time, see also Ralph Della Cava, "The 'People's Church,' the Vatican, and Abertura," in *Democratizing Brazil*, ed. Alfred Stepan (New York: Oxford University Press, 1989), pp. 143–67.

5   The chronology of events and the quotations that appear throughout this section are drawn from a content analysis of Brazil's most respected print media between 1986 and 1989. A list of the sources cited appears at the end of the Bibliography.

6   See Azevedo, *Basic Ecclesial Communities*, p. 254.

7   Interview with Dom Fernando Penteado, 2 June 1988.

8   Conferência Nacional dos Bispos do Brasil (CNBB), *Igreja: Comunhão e missão na evangelização dos povos, no mundo de trabalho, da política, e da cultura* (São Paulo: Paulinas, 1988), p. 94.

9   See Della Cava, "The People's Church"; and Doimo, "Social Movements and the Catholic Church," pp. 193–223.

Conclusion

1   See Gerth and Mills, eds., *From Max Weber*, pp. 283–84; and Barrington Moore, *Social Origins of Dictatorship and Democracy* (Boston: Beacon Press, 1966).

2   See Harvey Cox, *Religion in the Secular City* (New York: Simon and Schuster, 1984), chaps. 9, 10.

3   Adriance, "Opting for the Poor: A Socio-Historical Analysis," p. 144; Kevin Neuhouser, "The Radicalization of the Brazilian Catholic Church in Comparative Perspective," *American Sociological Review* 54 (April 1989): 239.

4   As reported in *Latin American Regional Reports—Brazil* (London), 14 September 1989, p. 5.

Bibliography

Books

Adriance, Madeleine. *Opting for the Poor: Brazilian Catholicism in Transition*. Kansas City, Mo.: Sheed and Ward, 1986.

Alves, Marcio Moreira. *A Igreja e a política no Brasil*. São Paulo: Brasiliense, 1979.

Ames, Barry. *Rhetoric and Reality in a Militarized Regime: Brazil since 1964*. Beverly Hills, Calif.: Sage, 1973.

Antoine, Charles. *Church and Power in Brazil*. Translated by Peter Nelson. London: Sheed and Ward, 1973.

Archdiocese of São Paulo. *3º plano bienal de pastoral, 1981–1983*. São Paulo: Archdiocese of São Paulo, 1981.

———. *5º plano bienal de pastoral, 1987–1990*. São Paulo: Archdiocese of São Paulo, 1987.

———. *Brasil: Nunca mais*. Petrópolis, RJ.: Vozes, 1985.

———. *Guia geral da arquidiocese de São Paulo, 1980*. São Paulo: Archdiocese of São Paulo, 1980.

———. *Guia geral da arquidiocese de São Paulo, 1983*. São Paulo: Archdiocese of São Paulo, 1983.

Arns, Paulo Evaristo Cardeal. *Em favor do homem*. Rio de Janeiro: Avenir, 1979.

Aron, Raymond. *The Opium of the Intellectuals*. Translated by Terrence Kilmartin. London: Secker and Warburg, 1957.

Azevedo, Fernando de C. *Canaviais e engenhos na vida política do Brasil*. São Paulo: Edições Melhoramentos, 1958.

Azevedo, Marcello de. *Basic Ecclesial Communities in Brazil: The Challenge of a New Way of Being Church*. Washington, D.C.: Georgetown University Press, 1987.

Baldissera, Adelina. *CEBs: Poder, nova sociedade*. São Paulo: Paulinas, 1988.

Baraglia, Mariano. *Evolução das comunidades eclesiais de base*. Petrópolis, RJ.: Vozes, 1974.

Barreiro, Alvaro. *Basic Ecclesial Communities*. Translated by Barbara Campbell. Maryknoll, N.Y.: Orbis, 1982.

Barros, Raimundo Caramuru de. *Comunidade eclesial de base: Uma opção pastoral decisiva*. Petrópolis, RJ.: Vozes, 1967.

Betto, Frei. *CEBs: Rumo a nova sociedade*. São Paulo: Paulinas, 1983.

————. *O que é comunidade eclesial de base?* São Paulo: Brasiliense, 1981.

Bittencourt, Getúlio, and Sergio Markum. *Dom Paulo Evaristo Arns: O cardeal do povo.* São Paulo: Alfa-Omega, 1979.

Boff, Clodovis. *Comunidade eclesial, comunidade política.* Petrópolis, RJ.: Vozes, 1978.

Bottomore, T. B., ed., *Karl Marx: Early Writings.* London: C. A. Watts, 1963.

Bourne, R. *Getúlio Vargas of Brazil: 1883–1954.* London: Charles Knight and Co., 1974.

Brazil-Canada Chamber of Commerce (BCCC). *Background on Brazil.* Toronto: Brazil-Canada Chamber of Commerce, 1982, 1986.

Bruneau, Thomas C. *The Catholic Church and the Basic Christian Communities: A Case Study from the Brazilian Amazon.* Discussion Paper Series, no. 7. Montreal: Centre for Developing-Area Studies, McGill University, 1983.

————. *The Church in Brazil.* Austin: University of Texas Press, 1982.

————. *The Political Transformation of the Brazilian Catholic Church.* London: Cambridge University Press, 1974.

Camargo, Cândido Procópio Ferreira de. *Igreja e desenvolvimento.* São Paulo: Editora Brasileira de Ciências, 1971.

Centro de Estatística Religiosa e Investigações Sociais (CERIS). *Anuário Católico.* Rio de Janeiro: CERIS, 1977.

Cleary, Edward. *Crisis and Change: The Church in Latin America Today.* Maryknoll, N.Y.: Orbis, 1985.

Comissão Arquidiocesana de Pastoral dos Direitos Humanos e Marginalizados de São Paulo (CAPDH). *Fé e política.* Petrópolis, RJ.: Vozes, 1981.

Conferência Nacional dos Bispos do Brasil (CNBB). *Igreja no Brasil, 1984.* Brasília: CNBB, 1984.

————. *Comunidades eclesiais de base na Igreja do Brasil.* Documentos da CNBB. São Paulo: Paulinas, 1983.

————. *Diretrizes gerais da ação pastoral da Igreja no Brasil, 1987–1990.* Documentos da CNBB. São Paulo: Paulinas, 1983.

————. *Diretrizes gerais da ação pastoral da Igreja no Brasil, 1987–1990.* Documentos da CNBB. São Paulo: Paulinas, 1987.

————. *Igreja: Comunhão e missão na evangelização dos povos, no mundo de trabalho, da política, e da cultura.* Documentos da CNBB. São Paulo: Paulinas, 1988.

————. *Comunidades eclesiais de base no Brasil.* Estudos da CNBB. São Paulo: Paulinas, 1981.

————. *Comunidades: Igreja na base.* Estudos da CNBB. São Paulo: Paulinas, 1977.

Cox, Harvey. *Religion in the Secular City.* New York: Simon and Schuster, 1984.

————. *The Secular City.* New York: Macmillan, 1965.

Empresa Metropolitana de Planejamento da Grande São Paulo (EMPLASA). *Sumário de dados da grande São Paulo.* São Paulo: EMPLASA, 1982, 1984, 1985, 1986, 1987.

Erickson, Kenneth. *The Brazilian Corporative State and Working-Class Politics.* Berkeley: University of California Press, 1977.

Faoro, Raimundo. *Os donos do poder.* Pôrto Alegre, RS.: Globo, 1976.

Ferm, Deane W. *Third World Liberation Theologies.* Maryknoll, N.Y.: Orbis, 1986.

Flynn, Peter. *Brazil: A Political Analysis.* London: Ernest Benn, 1978.

Follmann, José Ivo. *Igreja, ideologia, e classes sociais.* Petrópolis, RJ.: Vozes, 1985.

Freire, Paulo. *The Pedagogy of the Oppressed.* Translated by Myra Bergman Ramos. New York: Seabury Press, 1970.

Freyre, Gilberto. *The Mansions and the Shanties*. Translated by Harriet de Onis. New York: Alfred A. Knopf, 1966.

Gallet, Paul. *Freedom to Starve*. London: Gill and Macmillan, 1970.

Galletta, Ricardo et al., eds. *Pastoral popular e política partidária*. São Paulo: Paulinas, 1986.

Gerth, H. H., and C. Wright Mills, eds. *From Max Weber: Essays in Sociology*. New York: Oxford University Press, 1946.

Governo do Estado de São Paulo (GESP). *Subdivisão do município de São Paulo em áreas homogêneas*. São Paulo: Secretaria de Economia e Planejamento, Governo do Estado de São Paulo, 1977.

Gramsci, Antonio. *Selections from Political Writings*. Translated and edited by Quinton Hoare. London: Lawrence and Wishart, 1978.

Gregory, Afonso, and Maria A. Ghisleni. *Chances e desafios das comunidades eclesiais de base*. Petrópolis, RJ.: Vozes, 1979.

Guimarães, Almir Ribeiro. *Comunidades de base no Brasil*. Petrópolis, RJ.: Vozes, 1978.

Hewlett, Sylvia. *The Cruel Dilemmas of Development: Twentieth Century Brazil*. New York: Basic Books, 1980.

Hoornaert, Eduardo. *Formação do Catolicismo Brasileiro: 1500–1800*. Petrópolis, RJ.: Vozes, 1974.

Instituto Brasileiro de Geografia e Estatística (IBGE). *Anuário estatístico do Brasil*. Rio de Janeiro: Fundação IBGE, 1982, 1986.

———. *IX recenseamento geral do Brasil, 1980*, vol. 3, no. 17. Censo demográfico: Dados distritais, São Paulo. Rio de Janeiro: FIBGE, 1980.

———. *IX recenseamento geral do Brasil, 1980*, vol. 4, no. 19. Censo demográfico: Dados Gerais-migracão-instrução-fecundidade-mortalidade, São Paulo. Rio de Janeiro: FIBGE, 1980.

———. *IX recenseamento geral do Brasil, 1980*, vol. 5, no. 19. Censo demográfico: Familías e domicílios, São Paulo. Rio de Janeiro: FIBGE, 1980.

———. *IX recenseamento geral do Brasil, 1980*, vol. 6, no. 19. Censo demográfico: Familías e domicílios, São Paulo. Rio de Janeiro: FIBGE, 1980.

Kadt, Emanuel de. *Catholic Radicals in Brazil*. London: Oxford University Press, 1970.

Krischke, Paulo, and Scott Mainwaring, eds. *A Igreja nas bases em tempo de transição, 1974–1985*. São Paulo: L & PM Editores, 1986.

Levine, Daniel H., ed. *Churches and Politics in Latin America*. Beverly Hills, Calif.: Sage, 1979.

———, ed. *Religion and Political Conflict in Latin America*. Chapel Hill: University of North Carolina Press, 1986.

Lima, Luiz Gonzaga de Souza. *Evolução política dos Católicos e da Igreja no Brasil*. Petrópolis, RJ.: Vozes, 1979.

Lipset, Seymour M., and Aldo Solari, eds. *Elites in Latin America*. New York: Oxford University Press, 1967.

Maduro, Otto. *Religion and Social Conflicts*. Translated by Robert R. Barr. Maryknoll, N.Y.: Orbis, 1982.

Mainwaring, Scott. *The Catholic Church and Politics in Brazil, 1916–1985*. Stanford: Stanford University Press, 1986.

Mainwaring, Scott, and Alexander Wilde, eds. *The Progressive Church in Latin America*. Notre Dame: University of Notre Dame Press, 1989.

Mannheim, Karl. *Ideology and Utopia*. New York: Harcourt, Brace and World, 1936.

McCann, Dennis. *Christian Realism and Liberation Theology*. Maryknoll, N.Y.: Orbis, 1981.

Medina, Carlos Alberto de. *Participação e Igreja*. Petrópolis, RJ.: Vozes, 1971.

Michels, Robert. *Political Parties*. New York: Free Press, 1962.

Moore, Barrington. *Social Origins of Dictatorship and Democracy*. Boston: Beacon Press, 1966.

Pontifícia Comissão Justiça e Paz (PCJP). *São Paulo: Growth and Poverty*. London: Bowerdean Press, 1978.

Prefeitura do Município de São Paulo (PMSP). *Projeção da população do município de São Paulo por micro-area: 7º relatório*. São Paulo: PMSP, Coordenadora Geral de Planejamento, 1980.

Roett, Riordan. *Brazil: Politics in a Patrimonial State*. Boston: Allyn and Bacon, 1972.

Romano, Roberto. *Brasil: Igreja contra Estado*. São Paulo: Kairós Livraria e Editora, 1979.

Rubenstein, Richard, and John Roth, eds. *The Political Significance of Latin American Liberation Theology*. Washington, D.C.: Washington Institute Press, 1988.

Santayana, Mauro. *No meio do povo—Perfil biográfico de Dom Paulo Evaristo Arns*. São Paulo: Editora Salesiana Dom Bosco, 1983.

Schmitter, P.C. *Interest Conflict and Political Change in Brazil*. Stanford: Stanford University Press, 1971.

Segundo, Juan Luis. *The Hidden Motives of Pastoral Action*. Translated by John Drury. Maryknoll, N.Y.: Orbis, 1978.

Skidmore, Thomas E. *Politics in Brazil: 1930–64*. New York: Oxford University Press, 1967.

Stepan, Alfred, ed. *Authoritarian Brazil*. New Haven: Yale University Press, 1973.

———, ed. *Democratizing Brazil*. New York: Oxford University Press, 1989.

Tocqueville, Alexis de. *Democracy in America*. Vols. 1 and 2. Translated by Henry Reeve. New York: Random House, 1945.

Torres, Sergio, and John Eagleson, eds. *The Challenge of Basic Christian Communities*. Translated by John Drury. Maryknoll, N.Y.: Orbis, 1981.

Weber, Max. *The Protestant Ethic and the Spirit of Capitalism*. New York: Charles Scribner's Sons, 1958.

———. *Theory of Social and Economic Organization*. Translated by Talcott Parsons. New York: Free Press, 1946.

Willems, Emilio. *Followers of the New Faith*. Nashville: Vanderbilt University Press, 1968.

Articles

Adriance, Madeleine. "Opting for the Poor: A Social-Historical Analysis of the Changing Brazilian Catholic Church." *Sociological Analysis* 46 (Summer 1985): 131–46.

Alvarez, Sonia. "Politicizing Gender and Engendering Democracy." In *Democratizing Brazil*, edited by Alfred Spepan. New York: Oxford University Press, 1989.

Arns, Paulo Evaristo Cardeal. "Entrevista do cardeal de São Paulo ao jornal 'Movimento.' " *SEDOC* 12 (June 1980): 1212–27.

———. "Resposta de Dom Paulo Evaristo, Cardeal Arns, às questões de Claudio Viezzoli e Carlo Tassara, do 'Comitato Internazionale per 1º Sviluppo Dei Popoli.' " *SEDOC* 15 (May 1983): 1128–32.

Ávila, Fernando B. de. "A Igreja na crise Brasileira." *Síntese* 28 (May–July 1983): 7–24.

Betto, Frei. "As comunidades eclesiais de base como potencial de transformação da sociedade Brasileira." *Revista eclesiástica Brasileira* 43 (September 1983): 494–503.

———. "Oracão, uma exigência também política." *Revista eclesiástica Brasileira* 42 (September 1982): 444–55.

Bishops of São Paulo. "A Palavra de Deus e as comunidades eclesiais de base." 1982.

Boff, Clodovis. "Agente de pastoral e povo." *Revista eclesiástica Brasileira* 40 (June 1980): 216–41.

———. "CEBs e práticas de libertação." *Revista eclesiástica Brasileira* 40 (December 1980): 595–625.

———. "Em que ponto estão hoje as CEBs?" *Revista eclesiástica Brasileira* 46 (September 1986): 527–38.

———. "A influência política das comunidades eclesiais de base (CEBs)." *Religião e sociedade* 4 (1979): 95–120.

———. "Santo Tomás de Aquino e a teologia da libertação." *Revista eclesiástica Brasileira* 41 (September 1981): 426–42.

Boff, Clodovis, and Leonardo Boff. "Comunidades Cristãs e política partidária." *Revista eclesiástica Brasileira* 38 (September 1978): 387–401.

Boff, Leonardo. "CEBS: A Igreja inteira na base." *Revista eclesiástica Brasileira* 43 (September 1983): 459–69.

———. "Comunidades eclesiais de base: Povo oprimido que se organiza para a libertação." *Revista eclesiástica Brasileira* 41 (June 1981): 312–20.

———. "Igreja, povo que se liberta." *Revista eclesiástica Brasileira* 38 (September 1978): 503–11.

———. "Theological Characteristics of a Grassroots Church." In *The Challenge of Basic Christian Communities*, edited by Sergio Torres and John Eagleson. Translated by John Drury. Maryknoll, N.Y.: Orbis, 1981.

Bruneau, Thomas C. "Basic Christian Communities in Latin America: Their Nature and Significance (Especially in Brazil)." In *Churches and Politics in Latin America*, edited by Daniel H. Levine. Beverly Hills, Calif.: Sage, 1979.

———. "Brazil: The Catholic Church and Basic Christian Communities." In *Religion and Political Conflict in Latin America*, edited by Daniel H. Levine. Chapel Hill: University of North Carolina Press, 1986.

———. "Church and Politics in Brazil: The Genesis of Change." *Journal of Latin American Studies* 17 (1985): 271–93.

Bruneau, Thomas C., and W. E. Hewitt. "Patterns of Church Influence in Brazil's Political Transition." *Comparative Politics* 22 (October 1989): 39–61.

Camargo, Candido Procópio Ferreira de. "A Igreja do povo." *Novos estudos CEBRAP* 2 (April 1982): 49–53.

Camargo, Candido Procópio Ferreira de, Beatriz Muniz de Souza, and Antônio Flávio de Oliveira Pierucci. "Comunidades eclesiais de base." In *São Paulo: O povo em movimento*, edited by P. Singer and V. Brant. Petrópolis, RJ.: Vozes, 1980.

Cardoso, Ruth. "Duas faces de uma experiência." *Novos estudos CEBRAP* 2 (April 1982): 53–58.

Castanho, Dom Amaury. "Caminho das CEBs no Brasil." *Revista eclesiástica Brasileira* 46 (September 1986): 663–65.

Codina, Victor. "Eclesiologia Latino-Americana da libertação." *Revista eclesiástica Brasileira* 42 (March 1982): 61–81.

Cunha, Rogério de Almeida. "Consciência crítica." *Revista eclesiástica Brasileira* 40 (June 1980): 243–51.

———. "Teologia da libertação e pedagogia libertadora." *Revista eclesiástica Brasileira* 42 (March 1982): 143–54.

Dale, Romeu. "Da Ação Católica a opção pelos pobres." *SEDOC* 12 (May 1980): 1125–28.

Deelen, Gottfried. "The Church on Its Way to the People: Basic Christian Communities in Brazil." *Cross Currents* 30 (1980): 385–408.

Della Cava, Ralph. "Igreja e Estado no Brasil do Seculo XX: Sete mongrafias recentes sobre o Catolicismo Brasileiro, 1916–64." *Estudos CEBRAP* 12 (April–June 1975): 5–52.

———. "The 'People's Church,' the Vatican, and Abertura." In *Democratizing Brazil*, edited by Alfred Stepan. New York: Oxford University Press, 1989.

Demo, Pedro, and Elizeu F. Calsing. "Relatório da pesquisa sobre CEBs." In Conferência Nacional dos Bispos do Brasil (CNBB), *Comunidades: Igreja na base*. São Paulo: Edições Paulinas, 1977.

Doimo, Ana Maria. "Social Movements and the Catholic Church in Vitória, Brazil." In *The Progressive Church in Latin America*, edited by Scott Mainwaring and Alexander Wilde. Notre Dame: University of Notre Dame Press, 1989.

Dussell, Enrique. "Current Events in Latin America (1972–1980)." In *The Challenge of Basic Christian Communities*, edited by Sergio Torres and John Eagleson. Translated by John Drury. Maryknoll, N.Y.: Orbis, 1981.

Elhe, Paulo. "Formação de Animadores populares: Uma Avaliação." *Revista eclesiástica Brasileira* 44 (June 1984): 381–84.

Elias, Roseli. "CEBs: Movimento de base da Igreja ou popular?" *Cadernos do CEAS* 69 (1980): 47–53.

Fernandes, Dom Luis Gonzaga. "Gênese, dinâmica e perspectiva das CEBs do Brasil." *Revista eclesiástica Brasileira* 42 (September 1982): 456–64.

Fero, Cora. "The Latin American Woman: The Praxis and Theology of Liberation." In *The Challenge of Basic Christian Communities*, edited by Sergio Torres and John Eagleson. Translated by John Drury. Maryknoll, N.Y.: Orbis, 1981.

Follmann, José Ivo. "Espelho da sociedade de classes." *Parlamento* (1974) (1986): 26–28.

Fulton, John. "Religion and Politics in Gramsci: An Introduction." *Sociological Analysis* 48, no. 3 (1987): 197–216.

Gay, Robert. "Neighborhood Associations and Political Change in Rio de Janeiro." *Latin American Research Review* 25, no. 1 (1990): 102–18.

Gilpin, Robert G. "Development and Underdevelopment: Conflicting Perspectives on the Third World." In *Philosophy, History and Social Action*, edited by Sidney Hook, William L. O'Neill, and Roger O'Toole. Dordrecht, Boston, and London: Kluwer Academic Publishers, 1988.

Goldsmit, Shulamit, and Ernest S. Sweeney. "The Church and Latin American Women in Their Struggle for Equality and Justice." *Thought* 63 (June 1988): 176–88.

Gomes, Gilberto. "A autoconsciência eclesial do leigo nas CEBs." *Revista eclesiástica Brasileira* 43 (September 1983): 513–32.

Gregory, Afonso. "Dados préliminares sobre experiências de comunidades eclesiais de base no Brasil." In *Comunidades eclesiais de base: Utopia ou realidade?*, edited by Afonso Gregory. Petrópolis, RJ.: Vozes, 1973.

———. "Comunidades eclesiais de base: Busca de equilibrio entre ministérios e comunidade Cristã." *Revista eclesiástica Brasileira* 38 (March 1978): 80–102.

Gutiérrez, Gustavo. "The Irruption of the Poor in Latin America and the Christian Communities of the Common People." In *The Challenge of Basic Christian Communities*, edited by Sergio Torres and John Eagleson. Translated by John Drury. Maryknoll, N.Y.: Orbis, 1981.

Hewitt, W. E. "The Influence of Social Class on Activity Preferences of Comunidades Eclesiais de Base (CEBs) in the Archdiocese of São Paulo." *Journal of Latin American Studies* 19 (May 1987): 141–56.

———. "Liberation Theology as Social Science: Contributions and Limitations." In *Sociological Studies in Roman Catholicism*, edited by Roger O'Toole. Lewiston, N.Y.: Mellen, 1989.

———. "Origins and Prospects of the Option for the Poor in Brazilian Catholicism." *Journal for the Scientific Study of Religion* 28 (June 1989): 120–35.

———. "Strategies for Social Change Employed by Comunidades Eclesiais de Base (CEBs) in the Archdiocese of São Paulo." *Journal for the Scientific Study of Religion* 25 (March 1986): 16–30.

Hoornaert, Eduardo. "Comunidades de base: Dez anos de experiência." *Revista eclesiástica Brasileira* 38 (September 1978): 474–502.

———. "Os três fatores da nova hegemonia dentro da Igreja Católica no Brasil: Fatos e perspectivas." *Revista eclesiástica Brasileira* 26 (June 1986): 371–84.

Hummes, Cláudio, and Frei Betto. "A Igreja e a greve do ABC." *Revista eclesiástica Brasileira* 40 (December 1980): 721–28.

Ireland, Rowan. "Catholic Base Communities, Spiritist Groups, and the Deepening of Democracy in Brazil." In *The Progressive Church in Latin America*, edited by Scott Mainwaring and Alexander Wilde. Notre Dame: University of Notre Dame Press, 1989.

Kadt, Emanual de. "Religion, the Church and Social Change in Brazil." In *The Politics of Conformity in Latin America*, edited by Claudio Veliz. London: Oxford University Press, 1967.

Levine, Daniel H. "Colombia: The Institutional Church and the Popular." In *Religion and Political Conflict in Latin America*, edited by Daniel H. Levine. Chapel Hill: University of North Carolina Press, 1986.

———. "Popular Groups, Popular Culture, and Popular Religion." Working Paper No. 127. Helen Kellogg Institute for International Studies, University of Notre Dame, Notre Dame, Indiana (August 1989).

———. "Religion, the Poor, and Politics in Latin America Today." In *Religion and Political Conflict in Latin America*, edited by Daniel H. Levine. Chapel Hill: University of North Carolina Press, 1986.

Libânio, J. B. "CEBs: Igreja em busca da terra prometida." *Revista eclesiástica Brasileira* 46 (September 1986): 489–511.

———. "Igreja: Povo oprimido que se organiza para a libertação." *Revista eclesiástica Brasileira* 41 (June 1981): 279–311.

Mainwaring, Scott. "Grassroots Catholic Groups and Politics in Brazil." In *The Progressive Church in Latin America*, edited by Scott Mainwaring and Alexander Wilde. Notre Dame: University of Notre Dame Press, 1989.

Mainwaring, Scott, and Alexander Wilde. "The Progressive Church in Latin America: An Interpretation." In *The Progressive Church in Latin America*, edited by Scott Mainwaring and Alexander Wilde. Notre Dame: University of Notre Dame Press, 1989.

Marx, Karl. "On the Jewish Question." In *Karl Marx: Early Writings*, edited by T. B. Bottomore. London: C. A. Watts, 1963.

———. "Theses on Feuerbach." In *Marx and Engels: Basic Writings on Politics and Philosophy*, edited by Lewis S. Feuer. Garden City, N.J.: Anchor, 1959.

Melo, Antonio Alves G. "Classe média e Opção Preferencial pelos Pobres." *Revista eclesiástica Brasileira* 43 (June 1983): 340–50.

Michel, Irmão. "Comunidades Católicas de base são o fruto de colaboração entre duas classes sociais, a pobre e a média." *Revista eclesiástica Brasileira* 42 (March 1982): 120–28.

Moser, Antonio. "Aspectos morais da caminhada das CEBs no Brasil." *Revista eclesiástica Brasileira* 43 (September 1983): 504–12.

Neuhouser, Kevin. "The Radicalization of the Brazilian Catholic Church in Comparative Perspective." *American Sociological Review* 54 (April 1989): 233–44.

Oliveira, Pedro A. Ribeiro de. "O povo nas CEBs da arquidiocese de Vitória." *Revista eclesiástica Brasileira* 43 (March 1983): 93–102.

———. "Oprimidos: A opção pela Igreja." *Revista eclesiástica Brasileira* 41 (December 1981): 643–59.

Paiva, Vanilda. "A Igreja moderna no Brasil." In *Igreja e questão agrária*, edited by Vanilda Paiva. São Paulo: Loyola, 1985.

Palácio, Carlos. "Uma consciência histórica irreversivel (1960–1979: Duas décadas de história da Igreja no Brasil)." *Síntese* 17 (September–December 1979): 19–40.

Pastor, Felix Alexandre. "Paróquia e comunidade de base: Uma questão eclesiologica." *Síntese* 10 (May–August 1977): 21–45.

Perani, Cláudio. "Comunidades eclesiais de base e movimento popular." *Cadernos do CEAS* 75 (September–October 1981): 25–31.

Pierucci, Antonio Flávio de Oliveira. "Comunidades eclesiais: Origens e desenvolvimento." *Novos estudos CEBRAP* 2 (April 1981): 48–49.

Pretto, Hermilo E. "A eclesiologia das CEBs." *Vida pastoral*, July–August 1983, pp. 21–26.

Ramalho, Jether Pereira. "CEBs: Nova forma participatória do povo." Reproduced in *Comunidades eclesiais de base e movimento popular*. São Paulo: Centro Pastoral Vergueiro, 1983.

Repges, Walter. "The BCC and the Parish." In *Basic Christian Communities*. LADOC Keyhole Series. Washington, D.C.: Latin American Documentation, 1976.

Riley, Matilda White. "Aging, Social Change and the Power of Ideas." *Daedalus* 107 (Fall 1978): 39–52.

Rostow, W. W. "The Take-Off into Self-Sustained Growth." *Economic Journal*, March 1956, pp. 24–48.

Salem, Heléna. "As comunidades eclesiais, ou re-invenção da Igreja." In *A Igreja dos oprimidos*, edited by Antonio Carlos Moura et al. São Paulo: Editora Brasil Debates, 1981.

Sales, Eugenio de Araujo Cardeal. "Comunidades eclesiais de base." *Boletim da revista do clero*, September 1982, pp. 20–33.

Sanders, Thomas G. "The Catholic Church in Brazil's Political Transition." *American Universities Field Staff Reports* 48 (1980).

Sassatelli, Marcos. "Comunidades de base." Reproduced in *Comunidades eclesiais de base e movimento popular*. São Paulo: Centro Pastoral Vergueiro, 1983.

Sidney, Jairo Cesar, Oswaldo Truzzi, and Yone Moreira Fernandes. "Igreja e mobilização popular: As comunidades eclesiais de base." *Cadernos do CEAS* 75 (September–October 1981): 34–43.

Singer, Paul. "Movimentos de base." In *São Paulo: O povo em movimento*, edited by P. Singer and V. Brant. Petrópolis, RJ.: Vozes, 1980.

Skidmore, Thomas E. "The New Professionalism of Internal Warfare and Military Role Expansion." In *Authoritarian Brazil*, edited by Alfred Stepan. New Haven: Yale University Press, 1973.

Souza, Luiz Alberto G. de. "Igreja e sociedade: Elementos para um marco teórico." *Síntese* 13 (April–June 1978): 19–31.

Vallier, Ivan. "Religious Elites: Differentiations and Developments in Roman Catholicism." In *Elites in Latin America*, edited by Seymour Martin Lipset and Aldo Solari. New York: Oxford University Press, 1967.

Wanderley, Luiz Eduardo W. "Comunidades eclesiais de base (CEBs) e educação popular." *Revista eclesiástica Brasileira* 41 (December 1981): 686–707.

Theses, Dissertations, and Papers

Alvarez, Sonia. "Women's Participation in the 'People's Church': A Critical Appraisal." Paper presented at the 14th International Congress of the Latin American Studies Association, New Orleans, 17–19 March 1988.

Baraglia, Mariano. "Glória no Céu, poder na terra: Um estudo sobre vigários da grande São Paulo." Master's thesis, Universidade de São Paulo, 1983.

Beckford, James A. "Quasi-Marxisms and the Sociology of Religion." Paper presented at the Annual Meeting of the Society for the Scientific Study of Religion, Chicago, 28–30 October 1988.

Fernandes, Luiza. "Basic Christian Communities in the Brazilian Context." Paper presented at the Annual Meeting of the Society for the Scientific Study of Religion, Chicago, 26–28 October 1984.

Levine, Daniel H. "Popular Groups and Popular Culture." Paper presented at the Annual Meeting of the Society for the Scientific Study of Religion, Chicago, 28–30 October 1988.

Maduro, Otto. "Catholic Church, State Power, and Popular Movements." Paper presented at the Annual Meeting of the Society for the Scientific Study of Religion, Providence, R.I., 21–24 October 1982.

Mariz, Cecília. "Folk Religion, Basic Communities, and Pentacostalism in Brazil." Paper presented at the Annual Meeting of the Society for the Scientific Study of Religion, Chicago, 28–30 October 1988.

Newspapers and Magazines

Correio Braziliense (Brasília). Daily.
Folha de São Paulo (São Paulo). Daily.
Gazeta mercantil (São Paulo). Daily.
The Globe and Mail (Toronto). Daily.
O globo (Rio de Janeiro). Daily.
Isto é (São Paulo). Weekly.

Jornal do Brasil (Rio de Janeiro). Daily.
Latin American Regional Reports—Brazil (London). Quarterly.
Latin American Weekly Reports (London). Weekly.
O São Paulo (São Paulo). Weekly.
Veja (São Paulo). Weekly.

Index

Activities, CEB, 2, 7, 42–45, 46–49 pas-
sim, 74–77, 106–8, 116; preferences for,
45–46, 93–94; relationship to social
class, 68–70, 80, 107. See also *Con-
scientização* in CEBs; Membership, CEB;
Revindicações in CEBs
Adriance, Madeleine, x, 23, 57, 108
Almeida, Dom Luciano Mendes de, 34, 90,
96, 98–99, 101
Alvarez, Sonia, 63–64
Alves, Marcio Morreira, x
Araújo, Dom Serafim, 97
Arns, Cardinal Paulo Evaristo, 32–37 pas-
sim, 53–54, 67, 82–83, 98–101, 114. *See
also* São Paulo, archdiocese of
Azevedo, Marcello de, x, 6

Baldissera, Adelina, x, 8, 56
Baraglia, Mariano, 6
Barreiro, Alvaro, 7, 82
Base Christian community (Comunidade
Eclesial de Base, CEB): defined, 1, 6, 106,
113; types described, 46–47
Basic Education Movement (Movimento de
Educação na Base, MEB), 7, 97
Bauer, Bruno, 3
Bernardino, Dom Angélico Sândalo, 34,
67, 96
Betto, Frei, 8, 82
Boff, Clodovis, 8–9, 57, 84, 100, 109
Boff, Leonardo, 8, 21, 63, 82, 98, 100–101
Brazilian Communist Party (Partido Comu-
nista Brasileiro, PCB), 55, 89
Bruneau, Thomas C., x, 8–9, 20, 56

Calsing, Elizeu F., 8–10
Câmara, Dom Helder, 97, 101
Candomblé, 98
Capatan, Dom Joel, 55
Carter, Jimmy, 32
Casaldáliga, Dom Pedro, 101
Castanho, Bishop Amaury, 8
Catholic Action: in Brazil, 17, 22–25
passim; and CEBs, 25
Catholic Church. *See* Institutional Church,
Brazil; Roman Catholic Church
CEB. See Base Christian Community Cele-
brações, 43, 78
Center of Religious Research and Social
Investigations (Centro de Estatística
Religiosa e Investigações Sociais, CERIS),
7–8
Central-West Church, 18
CERIS. *See* Center of Religious Research
and Social Investigations
Charismatic renewal movement, 79, 89
CIMI. *See* Native Missionary Council
Citizenship, CEB enhancement of, 85–
87, 107. *See also Revindicações*; Social
change
Cleary, Edward, 8
CNBB. *See* National Conference of Brazilian
Bishops
Communist Party of Brazil, 97
Conflict: in CEB relationship with commu-
nity, 88; intra-CEB, 48–50, 89, 92, 94–95;
and pastoral agents' involvement with
CEBs, 58–59, 66, 88–89
Conscientização (Consciousness-raising,